CONTENTS

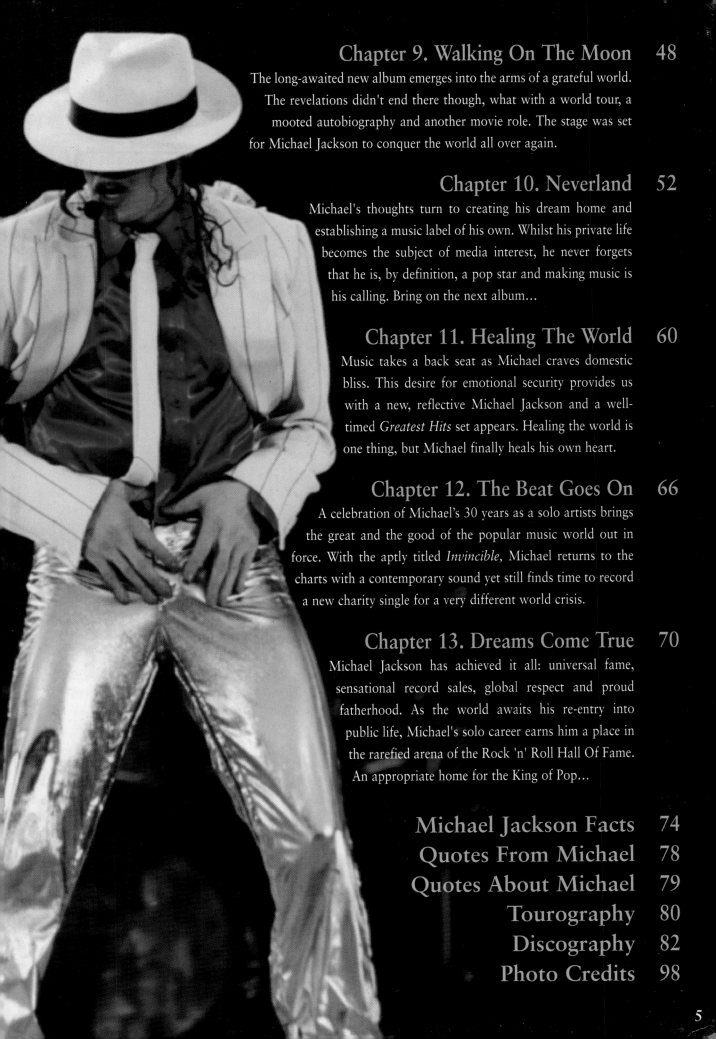

MICHAEL JACKSON
MODERN MAN

CHAPTER ONE
MODERN MAN

"When dancing, I felt touched by something sacred. In those moments I felt my spirit soar and become one with everything that exists. I became the stars and the moon. I became the lover and the loved. I became the victor and the vanquished...." It was with these grand words that Michael Jackson stormed into the 1990s, comprising as they did his personal sleeve note for the 1991 album, *Dangerous*. Upon first reading, they appear to be written by a man who maybe thought he had had his moment; as though popular culture was beginning to leave him behind. Of course, Jackson could be excused for thinking the Nineties were not the place for him. Previous decades had been kind: the Seventies had seen Michael, and his siblings, ride the wave of the soul-pop boom as The Jackson 5, to become one of the sensations of the era. The Eighties were equally generous to Michael as a solo artist. The record-buying public of the time had a huge appetite for pop music and consequently, Michael's songs found themselves a natural home.

By the end of the decade, however, the musical landscape was beginning to change and the world was now seemingly absorbed in rave culture. Those who had bought Michael Jackson records over the previous ten years were moving on and the music press were wondering whether there was a future for Michael and his particular brand of pop music. None of this appeared to worry Jackson though, and he would ultimately achieve what many would perceive to be the impossible - capture the zeitgeist whilst still forging his own, individual path. His ability to adapt to this shift in modern music surprised many. The hits continued to flow and Jackson proved that he was, beyond all doubt, a musical force to be reckoned with.

The albums he would release throughout the decade were as important as any with which he had made his name earlier in his career, containing everything anticipated of a Michael Jackson record: hard rocking beats sitting comfortably alongside gushing sentimentality; elements of insecurity giving way to moments of passionate air-punching, and all of this cocooned in the kind of sublime melodies one had come to expect from a record produced by any member of the talented Jackson clan. It all

Multi-Talented Michael
Singer
Composer
Lyricist
Poet
Producer
Arranger
Instrumentalist
Performer
Dancer
Choreographer
Actor
Director
Set Designer
Fashion Designer
Author

under-lined that Michael Jackson was still very much at the forefront of contemporary musical innovation.

In fact, it had always been like this. From the moment he started singing in the living room of the family home in a small suburb of Indiana, it was as if he had always been destined for greatness. Even at the tender age of five, he was performing with the impact of a great soul singer. The emotional situations which were the subject of his songs were beyond him, but his performance style was one of whole-hearted sincerity and totally mind-blowing to those fortunate enough to observe him at close quarters.

Whilst most five-year-olds were preparing themselves for the quantum leap from kinder-garten to elementary school, Michael - thanks to ambitious father Joe - was being groomed for an altogether bigger challenge: leading his band of brothers in the outfit that was to become a Seventies soul sensation: The Jackson 5.

MICHAEL JACKSON
CHILD STAR

CHAPTER TWO
CHILD STAR

Michael Joseph Jackson was born on August 29th, 1958, in the suburb of Gary, Indiana. He was born into a large family, the seventh child of Joseph Walter and Katherine Esther Jackson. They had married when Joseph was sixteen and although he dreamed of musical fame and fortune as a guitarist with his band The Falcons, he worked in the local steel industry as a crane operator. In order to bring extra money into the household, his wife worked part-time as a sales clerk for a local retail establishment in the family's hometown. Whilst Joseph had to sacrifice his own musical ambitions for a decent living wage to raise his ever-increasing family, it was still music that would prompt him to dramatically alter his career path in the late-Sixties, as his children were themselves to show an extraordinary natural gift for music and song.

Joseph still kept mementos from his days with

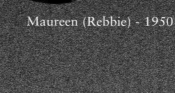

Marlon - 1957

Maureen (Rebbie) - 1950

Toriano (Tito) - 1953

Joseph Walter - 1929

Sigmund (Jackie) - 1951

12

The Falcons, particularly his precious guitar, and it was upon returning home one evening to find his second son, Tito, tinkering with the instrument that he first became aware of his children's talent. After administering a swift admonishment for tampering with the guitar without permission, Joseph was keen to see how well his son could play. To his surprise and delight, he could play very well indeed. His brothers Jackie and Jermaine soon accompanied Tito's guitar playing and it was suggested they should form as a group and play professionally.

The trio began to rehearse regularly and they recruited another brother, Marlon, but it was their mother who was to find the final piece in the jigsaw. She was becoming increasingly aware of young Michael's natural musical ability and she wasted no time in bringing it to the attention of her husband. Michael's pre-adolescent singing voice was fast developing into something special and, additionally, he was becoming proficient on the bongos. This was enough for Joseph to bring Michael into the fold and so he joined his elite band of brothers in practice sessions. In order to give his boys the best, Joseph bought as many instruments as his wage could afford and he even borrowed some from his cousins when money was tight.

Steven (Randy) - 1961

Janet - 1966

Michael - 1958

Katherine Esther - 1930

LaToya - 1956

Jermaine - 1954

Michael's talent was confirmed when he performed his first solo piece for a sc   ent. The number chosen was 'Climb Every Mountain' from the perennial movie fav   *The Sound of Music* and legend would record that his performance was stunning. N   was a mere five years old when he made his professional debut alongside his br   ow christened The Jackson 5, at a local Gary nightclub. Their pay for the evening   ltry eight dollars, but the band went down a storm and the crowd appreciatively th   ney on to the stage at the end of their performance, which amounted to more than c   red dollars.

As Michael turned 8 years old the group were performing on a regular basis,   n a major talent contest performing their rendition of The Temptations hit, 'M   The time Joseph was spending in taking care of the band's affairs was escalating,   were constantly travelling across the country to gigs and yet he was still working ful   the steel plant. He knew something had to give and he made the momentous dec   cut back on his hours at the plant, freeing up more time to focus upon his sons. I   wise decision as interest in his boys was continuing to rise. With the talent contest v   der their belts, word of mouth was beginning to promote The Jackson 5 and   nal bookings were becoming steady.

Ironically in spite of their constant travelling, it was back at home in Gary that they were to receive their first significant break. There was only one recording studio in the area, and it's owner, Keith Gordon, was becoming curious about these brothers who were now making noises both around town and far beyond. He arranged with

Joseph to see them perform at home and he immediately agreed to lend them his support after noticing the potential of their youngest member, Michael. Outside of his immediate family, Gordon was the first to notice Michael's leadership abilities and from here on in it was obvious that the youngster would be the focal point of the group.

Gordon took the band to his studio and they cut an R & B record, *Big Boy*, which was released in late 1967 on the independent Steeltown records and was a moderate hit in the local charts. It may have been cheap and cheerful, but the band was now committed to vinyl and it was only a matter of time before they were to become America's worst kept secret.

By the summer of 1968, their professional reputation had solidified and they were consistently playing The Regal Club in Chicago, where they opened for huge Motown acts such as Gladys Knight and The Pips and The Chi-lites. Now pushed to the forefront of the band, Michael was beginning to shine under the spotlight and revelled in becoming renowned as a mini James Brown. It was one of these performances at The Regal that would set them on the road to international success. Bobby Taylor, a popular record producer, saw that he had potential gold dust in front of his eyes and instantly told Joseph Jackson to load up the family Volkswagen - they were on their way to Detroit.

MICHAEL JACKSON
MOTOWN CALLING

MOTOWN CALLING

With their apprenticeship pretty much served, The Jackson 5 were on their way. The band's professional career had begun back home in Indiana, but it was about to explode in Detroit. The R & B influences, which had so informed their young lives and careers, were about to evolve into the rich, melodious sound of the Motown production line, their energy and natural musicianship welded together and honed for a record-buying public. The public was obviously ready for The Jackson 5 as records were bought by the truckload. Their debut single for Motown, *I Want You Back*, released in October 1969, was to become one of their most fondly remembered hits, slowly climbing to the top of the *Billboard* charts in January 1970.

It was also a massive world-wide smash, and the band were beginning to write a new chapter in the history of soul music as the five young boys from Indiana, led by the incredibly charismatic Michael, were fast becoming the new emblem for the Motown label.

They backed up this weighty responsibility with solid success: - *I Want You Back* was the first of four consecutive number one singles throughout 1970, an accomplishment that no artist before them had ever achieved. The incredible success of their first single naturally created huge anticipation for their debut album, and they were to have a very special fairy godmother to present their debut long-player to the public. An artist who had just achieved her twelfth number one hit for Motown and whose recommendation would no doubt guarantee maximum sales at the record counter. *Diana Ross Presents The Jackson 5* was released on 18th December 1969 and, as expected, was a huge success.

MICHAEL'S
LEAD VOCALS ARE
AMAZING

The album's opening track captured the very spirit of the band and of modern-day America. 'Zip A Dee Doo Dah' is a breezy, carefree, life-affirming number, and introduced the world to the versatile Jackson boys. This song led into an album of pure magic, it's centre-piece being the soulful ballad 'Chained'. Michael's lead vocals are amazing, employing a range of emotions unexpectedly wide for a boy of such tender years. His performance on this track drew comparisons to Marvin Gaye in terms of emotional delivery; a compliment of the highest order to any soul artist, but to a ten-year-old, a truly astonishing tribute to his innate talent. The album, although consisting mainly of covers, provided an opening three-track salvo that was to establish a recorded sound all of their own. The Jackson 5 were now a commercial force to be reckoned with.

Throughout the early Seventies, the band produced a prodigious amount of recorded material. In 1970 alone, they racked up three further number one singles with *ABC*, *The Love You Save* and *I'll Be There*, all of which featured on their two chart-topping albums, *ABC* and *Third Album*. They ended the year on a high note with the obligatory Christmas covers record, appropriately titled *The Christmas Album*. In the space of just fourteen months, The Jackson 5 had established a reputation for themselves as the young pretenders of modern soul music. Their performance skills were unimpeachable, their sales figures the envy of record company executives the world over and they were managed by the person closest to them - their father, Joe. They had the world very much at their feet and they consolidated their success with two further albums in 1971, *Maybe Tomorrow* and *Going Back To Indiana*.

Despite the continued success of the band as a whole, Motown executives were fully aware of the special talent of their front man, Michael. In 1970, MGM records launched The Osmonds in direct opposition to The Jackson 5, and expressed plans to promote their lead singer, 13 year-old Donny, as a future solo artist. It was a challenge to which Motown rose, believing they had the perfect response - Michael Jackson. Such was the success of The Jackson 5, though, Motown decided to rush-release a series of his solo material in conjunction with his band's output, making it a very busy 1972 for a young Michael Jackson.

Michael Jackson Number One *Billboard* Chart Singles

I Want You Back (The Jackson 5)

ABC (The Jackson 5)

The Love You Save I'll Be There (The Jackson 5)

Ben

Don't Stop Until You Get Enough

Rock With You

Billie Jean

Beat It

Say, Say, Say

We Are The World

I Just Can't Stop Loving You

Bad

The Way You Make Me Feel

Man In The Mirror

Dirty Diana

Black Or White

You Are Not Alone

CHAPTER 4

MICHAEL JACKSON
A NEW DIMENSION

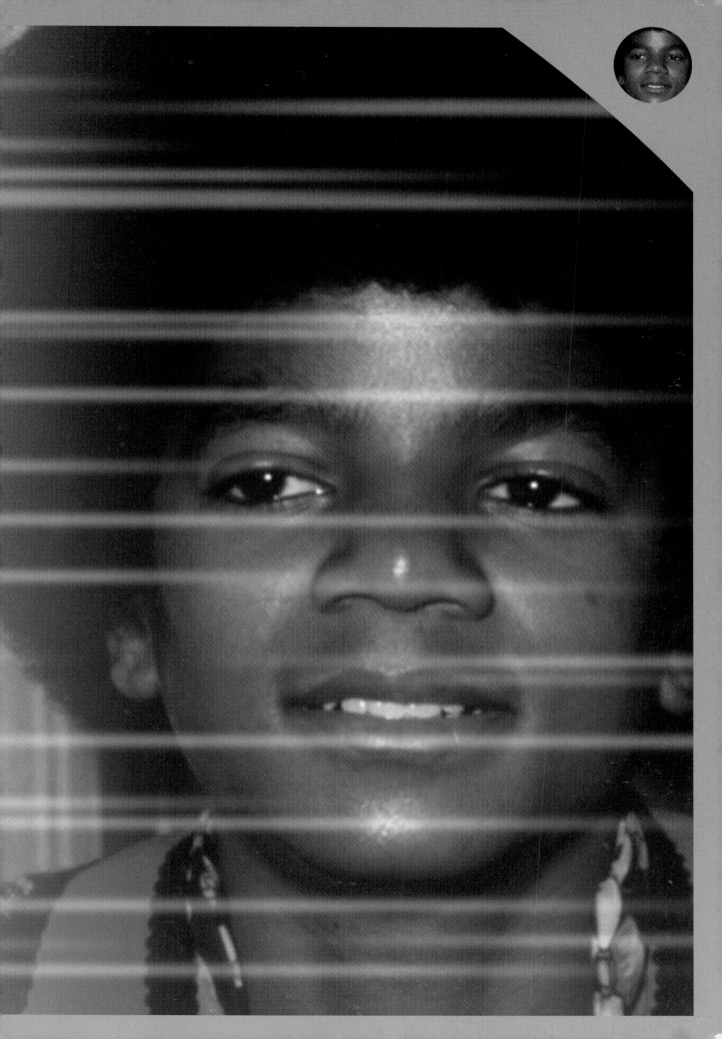

CHAPTER FOUR
A NEW DIMENSION

Michael Jackson the child star was amazing. His natural ability to perform in fro[nt] [l]arge audiences was phenomenal, betraying no nerves in singing either big ballads like ' [Love] You Save', or the more upbeat tunes such as the jubilant 'ABC'. However, he'd grow[n] [up] with his brothers performing behind him, and many wondered how he would cope on his [own.] The answer was simple - it was to be business as usual. Even at the age of 14, Michael sh[owed] no signs of being fazed by the solo career path that was offered to him as he set about [add]ing a new dimension to his work. His first release as a solo performer was the beautiful bal[lad] [']Got To Be There', a huge transatlantic hit, and he also got to number two with a versio[n] [of t]he rock 'n' roll novelty tune, 'Rockin' Robin'. An increased maturity was creeping into M[icha]el's performance style and this was crystallised on the series of solo recordings Motown [releas]ed between 1972 and 1973 to capitalise on Jackson's proliferating popularity.

'Got To Be There' was followed by 'Ben', the eponymous track being a supposed [lovin]g tribute to a pet rat. The song was released as a single, the title track to a new movie [and i]t climbed to number one. Michael Jackson was now a chart-topping artist all by him[self.] [A] further solo project, *Music and Me*, was released the following year and continued the [succes]s of his previous efforts. As these records were
released in conjunction with Jackson 5 material, the world was now wading knee deep in albums by the family. The solo material was particularly well received though, and their popularity ensured Michael was winning not only the hearts of millions of established Jackson 5 fans, but the respect of the music industry in general.

Meanwhile, Michael together with his brothers, was continuing to produce further career-consolidating records, releasing *Looking Through The Window* in 1972, *Skywriter* and *Get It Together* in 1973, but it

It's Only Skin Deep

If you look at any photo of Michael when he w[as] younger and compare it to photos of him today, [you] will clearly see that his skin was much darker in [the] past. Many columns of news print have been devot[ed to] the reasons for this but, far from artificially bleach[ing] his skin so he can look white, Michael actually ha[s a] rare dermatological condition called Vitiligo. This ca[uses] an irregular depigmentation of the skin, leaving suff[erers] with pale areas where the pigment has been lost. It [can] affect anyone at any time in their life and the medi[cal] profession do not fully understand why it happens.
Despite the fact that there are no other physical symptoms, the disorder can cause immense psychological distress because of the individual's cha[nge] in appearance. Like other sufferers, Michael wears ha[nd] masks, baggy clothes and makeup which cover his irregular skin tone. Although he was diagnosed in 198[6,] it was only in 1993 during his famous interview with Oprah Winfrey that he revealed it publicly.

was arguably their 1974 album *Dancing Machine* which marked a turning point for Mich[ael] as an individual. Whilst previous releases concentrated on the standard Motown confect[ion] delivered in Michael's appealing adolescent vocal styling, *Dancing Machine* gave [us] something different, something we had never heard before and something many would ido[lise] in later years: Michael's grown-up voice. The album was funky but chilled; it's high po[int] being the beautiful 'Forever Came Today'.

Michael was growing up, as were The Jackson 5 and their loyal fanbase. With the [...]se of their 1975 album, *Moving Violation*, came a sense of discontent with their lot at [...]own. Naturally, the album kept the cash tills ringing and the executives happy, but the [...] were beginning to strive for something more artistically satisfying. Despite a further so[...] oject that same year with *Forever, Michael*, which contained the elegantly languid, future [...] ingle *One Day In Your Life*, the end was in sight for The Jackson 5 and Motown. The[...] rded one more album for Berry Gordy's label, *Joyful Jukebox Music*, before the parting [...] ways became inevitable.

The band had decided that after 13 albums and innumerable top ten hit singles, th[...] was right for a move. Joe Jackson's talented boys were beginning to feel somewhat sti[...] y the

strict regime imposed upon them by Motown. The label refused to allow them to play their own instruments on record, nor were they offered the opportunity to choose the songs that made up their hit albums and, indeed, they were obliged to record songs that were not part of the Motown bank of hits. Their father negotiated a deal with Epic records, but the switch forced him to yield on two points. Firstly, Motown owned the rights to The Jackson 5 name and, perhaps in keeping with their growing maturity, the band were to become simply The Jacksons. The second concession was the loss of Jermaine who had married Hazel Gordy, the daughter of Motown chief Berry, and opted to stick with the label.

The label did not lose out entirely, owning, as they did, the entire Jackson 5 catalogue as well as hundreds of unissued recordings that they had stockpiled over the years. The move however, proved fruitful for the group and especially for Michael as it was under the auspices of Epic records that he was to secure a solo deal and make plans for a record-busting future.

CHAPTER 5

MICHAEL JACKSON
EPIC

CHAPTER FIVE
EPIC

And so gradually The Jackson 5 became just a pleasant memory, but the band was reborn and lived on simply as The Jacksons. The creative shackles so rigorously imposed upon the boys by Motown had been shaken off and they could now enjoy an element of artistic freedom proffered to them as part of their new deal with Epic. Following the success of his earlier releases, the label had serious intentions to launch Michael Jackson as a fully-fledged solo artist. But these were early days and such plans were temporarily put on hold whilst they marketed the brand new Jacksons. Joseph promoted his son Randy to the band on a full-time basis to compensate for the loss of Jermaine, and the boys began work on their first eponymously titled album for their new employers. The brothers undertook minor song-writing duties, contributing two songs to the album with the hugely successful partnership of Gamble and Huff overseeing the rest. The final product was a sophisticated record, yielding three minor hit singles, but is notable mainly for Michael's classy solo performance on the track 'Strength of One Man'. Their follow-up album again allowed them only two compositions of their own and the band, not to mention manager and father, were already becoming disillusioned, feeling as if they had swapped one straight-jacket at Motown for another with Epic. With this record, however, Michael's vocals were higher in the mix and it was becoming increasingly apparent that his solo career was just around the corner. The album's promotional singles charted only moderately and from then on, Joe and the band demanded that Epic loosen their creative grip on The Jacksons' music.

It was a victory well won and the band found themselves contributing more material to their records as well as taking over production duties. 'Shake Your Body To The Ground' was the centrepiece of their next album, *Destiny*, but it was the co-written 'Blame It On The Boogie' that was packing the dancefloors. The album featured four songs from the burgeoning writing team of Michael and brother Randy, and the set is noteworthy both for the development of Michael as a songwriter as well as it's heavy reliance upon his vocal work. The future was looking far more clear-cut for Michael Jackson. It was time to fly the nest.

Michael had accepted a major role in Sidney Lumet's film adaptation of L. Frank Baum's *The Wonderful Wizard Of Oz*. The film was to be a black adaptation of the fantasy story, Michael being cast as the scarecrow opposite Diana Ross' Dorothy. It was during the making of this film and it's soundtrack that he would establish a working relationship that would carry him into the next decade on a tidal wave of populist appeal. For it was here that Jackson was to meet a producer whose reputation went before him and whose body of work was mammoth and rich in quality. He was notable for his work in jazz music, on movie scores, in rock 'n' roll. He was to step into the realms of pop and funk, assisting as he did in creating the global superstar that was to be Michael Jackson. His name was Quincy Jones. He and Michael Jackson were about to make beautiful music together.

THE JACKSONS TODAY

Marlon and Jackie have become top media business men - Marlon has a gospel TV channel called MBC in Atlanta, while Jackie runs an internet company and has a share in the record company Modern Records. Tito manages his sons' group 3T, while Jermaine is involved in a variety of music industry projects. Although all the members have carved out new lives for themselves, for several years there have been rumours that The Jackson Five are working on a new album project. The working title for this project is J5 and all the members, including Michael, have been writing and recording material for it. As the individuals involved are very busy people, it has been difficult arranging a schedule where they can all get together at the same time. The Jacksons did reunite for Michael's September 2001 shows, marking 30 years as a solo artist, and gave some excellent performances, proving they have not lost any of the old magic.

CHAPTER 6

MICHAEL JACKSON
SUPERSTAR

SUPERSTAR

It had been four years since Michael had ventured into the solo arena with 1975's *Forever, Michael* and he could be forgiven for being less than confident in returning to the spotlight. For The Jacksons, the move to Epic records had not been a total success. The glory years of Motown were behind them and the flame failed to re-ignite with their new masters. Sales of their records were in decline as the musical world moved out of disco and into the punk era. Michael Jackson, though, had faith in his own abilities and in what he had to offer to the

Off The Wall (1979)
Total sales exceeded 15 million copies. The record was on the Billboard Pop Chart for 84 weeks, reaching a top position of number 3, and reached number 5 on the UK Album Charts.

Highest UK Single Chart Position
3 Don't Stop Til You Get Enough
3 She's Out Of My Life
7 Rock With You
7 Off the Wall
41 Girlfriend
Highest US Single Chart Position
1 Don't Stop Til You Get Enough
1 Rock With You
10 Off The Wall
10 She's Out Of My Life

public. The Jacksons might still be a living, breathing entity, but the time was right for the world to be introduced to Michael Jackson, solo artist.

Following his stint on the Sidney Lumet movie, Michael set about some serious songwriting and he delivered a batch of impressive songs. He was considering producing his own next solo record but decided against it, feeling his abilities in this area were not yet sophisticated enough to produce a complete album by himself. He called Quincy Jones for advice on potential producers for the project and he put the phone down having secured the ideal man - Jones offered his own services on the spot. Jones also immediately tracked down British songwriter he admired, Rod Temperton, member of the band Heatwave, and requested songs for Michael Jackson. After agreeing to contribute one track to the record, he flew out to Los Angeles and was so impressed by the project, he stayed on board for the entire production, eventually handing over three songs for the album, one of which became the title track, 'Off The Wall'. The stage was set for these three troubadours to begin inventing the sound of a new kind of modern soul music.

Michael was anxious to have this new project perceived as purely a Michael Jackson venture, rather than another Jacksons side project and there was a conscious effort on the part of all involved to produce something palpably different. Whilst the end product remains faithful to previous efforts in terms of clean and tidy production, the influence of Jones and Temperton ensured the versatility of Michael as an individual was raised a notch, introducing a new sophistication and maturity to Michael Jackson the adult performer. Certainly, *Off The Wall* sounds a lot different stylistically, combining driven dance tunes with dreamy ballads. The added ingredient, of course, was Michael's newly sagacious voice whilst remaining as flexible as ever. *Off The Wall* was released to a rapturous critical reception and was, unsurprisingly, a world-wide hit. The record was accompanied by four single releases which all went into the top ten, an unprecedented achievement at that time. Two of them, *Don't Stop 'Til You Get Enough* and *Rock With You*, both hit the top spot. The album sold millions, appealing to both Jacksons fans and legions of new followers. The future of Michael Jackson seemed secure.

After promoting *Off The Wall*, Michael returned to the studio to record a new album with his brothers. Spending studio time with Quincy Jones worked in Michael's favour as the Jacksons produced their best album in years. However, it was released shortly after *Off The Wall* and was unfortunately forced to live in the shadow of its predecessor, ensuring the album was chronically undervalued. This was testament, though, to Michael's increasing stature as a solo artist and what happened next would drop a bombshell upon the world of pop music. For when Michael and Quincy Jones reconvened in the studio to begin work on the follow-up to *Off The Wall*, little did they know they were to spawn a monster. Put simply, Jacksonmania was about to arrive.

CHAPTER 7

MICHAEL JACKSON
KING OF POP

KING OF POP

The 1980s were with us and Michael Jackson's new incarnation was winning him scores of new fans, whilst those who'd bought his records over the previous decade were adding his new material to their collections. Little did he know that he would thank them for their continued support with a record that would become one of the most commercially successful albums of all time. Jackson touched base once more with Quincy Jones and Rod Temperton and between them they created the record-busting *Thriller*. It would achieve more than 50 million world-wide sales and spend more than 37 weeks at number one in the *Billboard* album charts alone, longer than any other modern pop recording. *Thriller* produced seven top 10 hits, beating the record of four from a single album held by the likes of Bruce Springsteen and Fleetwood Mac, and this meant that Michael Jackson dominated the charts globally during the year of the album's release.

It's first single was a duet with Paul McCartney entitled *The Girl Is Mine* which peaked at number two in the charts. This was merely the warm-up though, as the follow-up single would send the *Thriller* album into orbit. It was a lukewarm start for the single when it

I Wrote That!

Given the widespread dissemination of Michael's music, the law of averages makes it inevitable that songwriters will see certain similarities between Jackson's compositions and their own work. As a result of this there have been several court cases taken out against Michael for copyright infringement. For example, he was sued by a Denver based songwriter called Crystal Cartier who claimed that 'Dangerous' had been stolen from one of her songs. Fortunately for Michael the court did not agree and upheld his defence that it was an original composition. Although similar claims have been made for 'The Girl Is Mine', 'We Are The World', 'Thriller', and 'Will You Be There' amongst others, Jackson and his legal advisors have won every case.

entered the top 100 at number 47, but six weeks later *Billie Jean* stood proudly at the top of the chart, giving Jackson the added distinction of becoming the first artist in *Billboard* chart history to have number one records simultaneously on both the black and pop charts. Jackson leapt a further barrier when the unique video to *Billie Jean*, in which Michael portrayed a powerful magician, became the first promo video by a black artist to be shown on MTV. The single remained at number one for seven weeks, and fans and critics alike praised the video. The rock-flavoured *Beat It* became the third single and took the same route to number one, producing another video that hooked fans. It was this innovative approach to the video medium that was to see the next single, the album's title track, sell in droves as the short film that accompanied it stunned the music industry with it's cinematic ambition. The song itself was a chunky slab of modern disco-funk, and the video was to become nothing short of a classic. Featuring Michael as a werewolf and associating with all manner of ghouls and zombies, it is a self-contained film clocking in at 14 minutes, the longest music video to date and also the first to feature closing credits.

Directed by movie mogul John Landis, an unprecedented $800,000 was spent on producing the film which scooped several awards including MTV's Best Video of the Eighties, 1984 People's Choice award for favourite video and the American Video Award for best direction. A full-length

Thriller (1982)
Total sales exceed 51 million copies. The record was number 1 on the Billboard Album Chart for 37 weeks, spending a combined total of 122 weeks on the chart. It was also number 1 in the UK album charts.

Highest UK Single Chart Positions
1 Billie Jean
3 Beat It
8 The Girl is Mine
9 Wanna Be Startin' Somethin'
10 Thriller
11 PYT
Highest US Single Chart Positions
1 Billie Jean
1 Beat It
3 Thriller
5 Wanna Be Startin' Something
7 Human Nature
10 P.Y.T.

video detailing the making of the *Thriller* promo was released and was to become one of the best selling home-videos ever made.

With such a fanfare surrounding the video, it would be easy for the quality of the music to be lost. However, it is a tribute to Michael Jackson's consummate musicianship that there is barely a weak moment on *Thriller* and the record is revered as a complete album, and not just for it's title track.

Further singles including *Pretty Young Thing*, *Human Nature* and *Wanna Be Startin' Somethin'* all sold well, and a further collaboration with Paul McCartney, *Say, Say, Say*

was such a huge hit, staying at the top of the US charts for six weeks, that *Thriller* was eventually updated to include the track, further increasing it's already phenomenal world-wide sales. Unsurprisingly, the album swept the board at the Grammy Awards in 1984. Michael was awarded seven gongs, including those for Best Album and Best Male Artist, and such was his impact upon current popular culture that he was awarded an eighth, for his narration on an album based on Steven Spielberg's hit movie, *E.T. - The Extra Terrestrial*.

Michael Jackson had reached the very pinnacle of his career. The accolades he had received as part of The Jackson 5 and The Jacksons now seemed a distant memory as his solo career swallowed everything whole. Of course, the question everybody wanted answering was what would be Michael Jackson's next move? After all, conquering the world is a difficult act to follow. The answer was simple - he could now do anything he wished.

'Q' and 'M'

Quincy Jones is one of the worlds greatest musical movers and shakers and has been intimately connected with the solo work of Michael Jackson both as producer and mentor. With an illustrious career that spans more than half a century, 'Q' has worked as a composer, record producer, instrumentalist, arranger, conductor, film and TV producer, record company executive, magazine founder, and multi-media entrepreneur. All of this activity has brought him 26 Grammy Awards, The Grammy Living Legend Award, an Emmy Award and seven Oscar nominations. He is also the most nominated Grammy artist ever with a total of 76 Grammy nominations, and remains one of the most successful and admired creative individuals in America today.

Born in Chicago in 1933, Jones grew up in Seattle where he learned to play the trumpet and flexed his vocal chords in a gospel choir. After studying at the Berklee College Of Music in Boston, he toured with various bands and, following a move to New York in 1951, started arranging and recording for a wide range of artists such as Sarah Vaughan, Count Basie, Duke Ellington and Frank Sinatra. In 1961, the 28 year old Quincy was appointed vice-president of Mercury records, an association with the business side of the music industry that continues to this day. In the early 1960's he started scoring film music and became one of the first black composers to be accepted by the Hollywood establishment, infusing his scores with the fresh sounds of soul and jazz.

In 1970, Quincy was attending a party at Sammy Davis Jr.'s house when he was first introduced to Michael Jackson. They became firm friends but it was not until they worked together on Sidney Lumet's 1978 film *The Wiz*, in which Michael played the scarecrow to Diana Ross' Dorothy, that they started a professional relationship too. When Michael came to work on his first post Jacksons solo album, *Off The Wall* he called Quincy to ask if he could recommend people to help him out. Within minutes of talking, Quincy decided that he wanted to do it himself and the rest is history. Although Michael had wowed the world as part of The Jackson Five, his future solo success wasn't that assured and Quincy found him, "Introverted, shy and nonassertive. He wasn't at all sure he could make a name for himself on his own. Neither was I". Although *Off The Wall* was well received, no one could have predicted the run away success of their next collaboration *Thriller* which became a record breaking release. He also worked on *Bad* with Jackson as well as producing the charity hit single *We Are The World*. Although Jackson and Jones have not worked together for some time, they still remain good friends and Michael often acknowledges the debt he owes Jones. As he wrote in the notes for *HIStory*, "Thank you Quincy for showing us the way. We love you madly..."

Although Quincy does not work with Michael any more he is still highly active. He runs his own company Qwest Records which has released work by artists such as New Order and Tevin Campbell as well as sound track albums for *Boyz N The Hood*, *Sarafina!* and *Malcolm X*. Quincy is also the driving force behind the NBC-TV hit series *The Fresh Prince Of Bel Air*, featuring film star and rapper Will Smith.

MICHAEL JACKSON
PERSONAL TOUCH

PERSONAL TOUCH

The rollercoaster that was *Thriller* could have allowed Michael Jackson to relax, put his feet up and bask in reflective glory. His strict work ethic though, a legacy from the punishing regime he endured throughout the early days of The Jackson 5, was not going to let him do that. Pepsi Cola had recognised Michael Jackson as a highly marketable product, and they signed him to a mammoth sponsorship deal, which was revealed to be the most lucrative in advertising history for a solo artist. Pepsi would see a comfortable return on the investment, as Michael's *Thriller* album was still selling across the globe and the variety of different projects he was planning would keep him very much in the public eye. The year of his ascent to the throne of King of Pop saw him regroup with his brothers for what was supposed to be a farewell album for The Jacksons. With music fans everywhere craving Michael Jackson material, the album *Victory* rocketed to number four on the *Billboard* charts, receiving double-platinum status, and the accompanying world tour quickly sold out. Unsurprisingly, considering his superstar status, the album's highlights are very much Michael-based. His duet with Mick Jagger on *State of Shock* was well received and the plaintive tracks, *One More Chance* and *Be Not Always* were part of a triumphant set of songs.

Following completion of the tour, Michael went home to contemplate his next move. At this time millions in Ethiopia were dying of starvation due to the combined effects of civil war and drought. The veteran entertainer

Belafonte decided that he would get together a group of other musicians and s and make a record that could be sold to raise money for alleviating the effects of the famine. He got in touch with an old friend Ken Kragen and er they started to pull in as many famous names as possible. They decided Quincy Jones would be the best person to produce and he in turn asked el Jackson and Lionel Richie to compose the song, which they did in January

THOSE WHO TOOK PART IN USA FOR AFRICA

Harry Belafonte, Lindsey Buckingham, Kim Carnes, Ray Charles, Bob Dylan, Sheila E., Bob Geldof, Hall and Oates, James Ingram, Jackie Jackson, LaToya Jackson, Marlon Jackson, Michael Jackson, Randy Jackson, Tito Jackson, Al Jarreau, Waylon Jennings, Billy Joel, Cyndi Lauper, Huey Lewis and the News, Kenny Logins, Bette Midler, Willie Nelson, Jeffery Osborne, Steve Perry, The Pointer Sisters, Lionel Richie, Smokey Robinson, Kenny Rogers, Diana Ross, Paul Simon, Bruce Springsteen, Tina Turner, Dionne Warwick, Stevie Wonder

ng 'We Are The World' was recorded after the American Music Awards in ngeles on the 28th of January 1985. A host of the USA's most popular ans and singers came together as USA For Africa at the A&M recording s in Hollywood to lay the song down. Released on March the 7th 1985, bia Records waived manufacturing and distribution fees and shipped 0 copies to record shops across the USA, all of which sold out within 48 making it the fastest selling single ever. Demand for the record was shing and it topped the charts across the globe for weeks, eventually selling han seven million copies in the United States alone. The money raised from ord totalled in the region of $60 million and was put to immediate use, with es being shipped to Africa just two months after the record hit the shops.

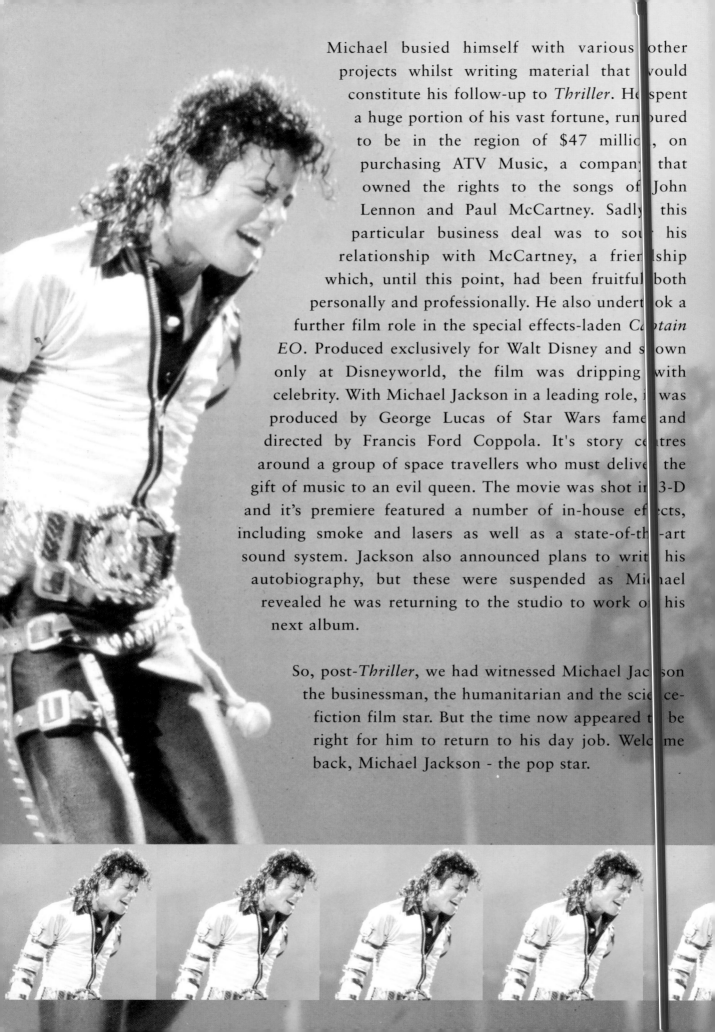

Michael busied himself with various other projects whilst writing material that would constitute his follow-up to *Thriller*. He spent a huge portion of his vast fortune, rumoured to be in the region of $47 million, on purchasing ATV Music, a company that owned the rights to the songs of John Lennon and Paul McCartney. Sadly this particular business deal was to sour his relationship with McCartney, a friendship which, until this point, had been fruitful both personally and professionally. He also undertook a further film role in the special effects-laden *Captain EO*. Produced exclusively for Walt Disney and shown only at Disneyworld, the film was dripping with celebrity. With Michael Jackson in a leading role, it was produced by George Lucas of Star Wars fame and directed by Francis Ford Coppola. It's story centres around a group of space travellers who must deliver the gift of music to an evil queen. The movie was shot in 3-D and it's premiere featured a number of in-house effects, including smoke and lasers as well as a state-of-the-art sound system. Jackson also announced plans to write his autobiography, but these were suspended as Michael revealed he was returning to the studio to work on his next album.

So, post-*Thriller*, we had witnessed Michael Jackson the businessman, the humanitarian and the science-fiction film star. But the time now appeared to be right for him to return to his day job. Welcome back, Michael Jackson - the pop star.

Jackson & McCartney

Michael Jackson and Paul McCartney have known each other since 1969, but only became very good friends in the late 1970's after McCartney had written the song 'Girlfriend' for Jackson's first solo album, *Off The Wall*. In the early 1980's they collaborated further with the song 'The Girl Is Mine' on *Thriller* and the single *Say Say Say* which was also released on Paul McCartney's solo album *Pipes Of Peace*.

In the mid-1980's, The Beatles song catalogue came up for sale, and both McCartney and Jackson decided to bid for it. The Beatles had originally assigned their music publishing to a company they partly owned called Northern Songs. In 1969 this was bought out by ATV who kept the songs until 1984 when they decided to sell their entire music catalogue. In addition to more than 200 songs by The Beatles, the catalogue contained over 4,000 songs penned by the likes of Elvis, Little Richard and Pat Benetar. At the time, McCartney just couldn't raise the money to buy the songs so it went to Jackson for the sum of 47 million dollars. Almost ten years later, Michael merged the catalogue with Sony Music Publishing earning many times what he had paid for it in the first place, as well as a stake in the new company.

The whole affair distressed McCartney who had allegedly asked Jackson to purchase the catalogue with him in partnership. Even now, McCartney is still annoyed about the events. In an interview on the *Howard Stern Show* in October 2001, he stated that Jackson "won't even answer my letters, so we haven't talked and we don't have that great a relationship". According to McCartney when he raised the matter with Jackson, he responded "Oh Paul, that's just business". If the catalogue does ever come up for sale again, and it is highly unlikely that it ever would, McCartney might not even be able to afford it as it's estimated worth is close to 180 million dollars.

CHAPTER 9

MICHAEL JACKSON
WALKING ON THE MOON

CHAPTER NINE
WALKING ON THE MOON

A game of Chinese whispers was gathering pace within the music industry. What would Michael Jackson's follow-up album to the monumentally triumphant *Thriller* be called? It was in September 1987, a full five years after his last entry into solo waters, that he would satisfy everyone's curiosity. The record was to be entitled *Bad*. There could not have been a less appropriate title for the disc as the music, contained within a sparse white sleeve with Michael in full macho repose, was anything but bad. The musical climate might have changed considerably, but Michael and Quincy Jones, once again on production duties, created another collection of songs within touching distance of anything on *Thriller*.

Another assault on the singles chart was expected of this album and it didn't disappoint, delivering five number one songs. It's flagship single was to be *I Just Can't Stop Loving You*, a duet with Siedah Garret, and the album's only real moment of poignant balladry, it's chart success was predictable. Further singles included *Man In The Mirror*, notable for it's anthemic chorus, the wonderfully melodramatic *Smooth Criminal*, and the title track, with Michael once again raising standards for video production with it's stunning promotional film.

Bad (1987)
Total sales exceeded 25 million. It debuted at number 1 on the Billboard Album Chart, spending 6 weeks at number one and 87 weeks on the chart. It also went to number 1 in the UK album charts.

Highest UK Single Chart Positions
1 I Just Can't Stop Loving You
2 Leave Me Alone
3 Bad
3 The Way You Make Me Feel
4 Dirty Diana
8 Smooth Criminal
11 Another Part Of Me
13 Liberian Girl
22 Man In The Mirror
Highest US Single Chart Positions
1 I Just Can't Stop Loving You
1 Bad
1 The Way You Make Me Feel
1 Man In The Mirror
1 Dirty Diana
7 Smooth Criminal
11 Another Part Of Me

Despite the album containing strong material, Michael refused to let the album speak for itself and insisted on undertaking a huge world tour to promote it. This was greeted by ecstatic fans world-wide and he played to more than half a million people in London alone, selling out seven nights at Wembley Stadium. The record sold in millions and is a sensational accomplishment considering the shadow cast over it by *Thriller*. Once Michael had caught his breath following an exhaustive world tour, his long-mooted autobiography finally made an appearance. Entitled *Moonwalk*, the book contained no great personal or artistic insight but, considering Michael Jackson's superstar status, had great commercial appeal. The book was launched in spectacular fashion and was accompanied by a full-length feature film, with the same name, released to catch the Christmas market in December 1988, and starring Michael himself as a crusader battling Joe Pesci's evil crime lord. The first thirty minutes of the film serve as an overview of Michael's career, from his adolescent days with The Jackson 5, right up to the date of his current album of the time. Jackson fans were naturally enthralled as they were given the opportunity to sit back and enjoy the music of their idol in the expansive surroundings of a movie theatre. The film was a modest success at the box-office, created as it was for Michael Jackson devotees, but it achieved the after-effect of selling more records and books. The video release of the movie was also expected to sell well, providing as it did the perfect piece of memorabilia to Jackson's career. The film bolstered his reputation as an original thinker in terms of music video and his commitment to the art was rewarded by MTV with their own Vanguard award. They were piling up elsewhere too, as *Bad* picked up a variety of trophies, including 3 *Billboard* Music Awards.

Michael And The Jehovah's Witnesses

Michael and his siblings were all brought up as Jehovah's Witnesses, following the conversion of their mother Katherine. As Michael grew older and more famous, he started coming into increasing levels of conflict with the church. He was constantly criticised for his appearance, and after he had cleaned up at the 1984 Grammy Awards, he was presented with an ultimatum - music or the church. Although the elders were also uncomfortable with the supernatural elements of the Thriller concept, it was their directions on his relationship with his sister La Toya that really made Michael rethink. Because she had stopped attending church meetings, the church decided that it would be better if Michael ceased contact with her until she returned to the fold. After much soul searching, Michael left the congregation for good in 1987.

The 1980s were almost at an end, a decade in which Michael Jackson had triumphed both artistically and financially. He had created the best-selling album of all-time, produced and starred in a ground-breaking music video and had become one of the world's most enigmatic pop stars. As the 80s drew to a close, was Michael Jackson ready for the 1990s? And, indeed, were the 1990s ready for him?

CHAPTER 10

MICHAEL JACKSON

NEVERLAND

WALKING ON THE MOO

If some music commentators thought *Bad* failed to reach the standards set predecessor his fanbase thought otherwise and the album was certified 6 times pla within a year of its release. Such astonishing sales confirmed Michael Jackson as an who continued to carry much influence in modern music, and this prompted Pepsi C offer him another multi-million dollar contract. The conglomerate secured him to a in four television commercials promoting their product for a staggering $12 m making him the highest paid commercial representative in advertising history. Musi already made him a millionaire many times over, but the corporate dollar substan inflated his already vast fortune, giving him a financial security that would have unthinkable in the days when he and his brothers performed in the family living room.

Dangerous (1991)
Total sales of just under 27 million. It debuted at number 1 on the Billboard Album Chart, spending four weeks at number one. It also went straight to number 1 in the UK Album Charts.

Highest UK Single Chart Positions
1 Black Or White
2 Heal The World
2 Give In To Me
4 Remember The Time
8 In The Closet
9 Will You Be There
10 Who Is It
12 Jam
33 Gone Too Soon

Highest US Single Chart Positions
1 Black Or White
3 Remember The Time
6 In The Closet
7 Will You Be There
14 Who Is It
26 Jam
27 Heal The World

1980s had been kind to him and, making money no longer a necessit was time for Michael to consider home life. He began by purcha Neverland Valley, a sprawling ranc California that he planned to con into his dream home. It would take y of development, but the estate wo eventually consist of a full-size mo theatre, an amusement park as well a zoo allowing Michael to indulge his lo of animals.

On the career front, *Bad* was st picking up awards. The single *Leave M Alone*, which was another internation hit, won a Grammy award for be music video. Michael also planned t establish his own record label with primary intention to sign promising R & acts. The label, MJJ Records, would sign bands such as 3T and Brownstone both of whom experienced a modicum of chart success. Michael Jackson the solo artist was also expected to make a swift return and Sony Music invested heavily in him, tying Michael to the largest ever recording contract in the history of the corporation. They were to be the grateful recipients of another blockbusting album as Michael planned a return to the charts at the end of 1991.

The album was to be called *Dangerous* and was, once again, laden with potential hit singles. The record was launched in Paris and it became an inevitable transatlantic number one. The content of *Dangerous* fell in perfectly with the popular music of the age, adding a dancefloor sensibility to his work that had previously based itself upon a traditional pop agenda. Despite a move into modern day dance music, the record still revealed the inevitable Jackson sound, which the lead-off single, *Black Or White*, summarises perfectly.

The track blends a political backbone, and its allusions to racism, with a sweet pop melody, a combination which guaranteed the single a number one spot as well as garnering many critical plaudits. Other singles followed, including *Remember The Time* and *Will You Be There*, the latter becoming the theme song for the hit movie, *Free Willy*. One of the most remarkable tracks is the lip-trembling 'Gone Too Soon', a moving tribute to Michael's friend Ryan White who tragically died at the age of 18. It was another hit single, *Heal The World*, which would provide Michael's next charitable venture with its very name.

The Heal The World Foundation was formed in 1992 by Michael himself, the organisation's brief being to aid under-privileged children and the environment. This included supplying much-needed medicine to sick children with the ultimate goals of tackling world famine and drug abuse. Heal The World is an umbrella organisation under which a number of established groups provide expertise in helping realise these goals. During its first year alone, the consortium was able to fly 47 tons of winter relief, such as medical items, blankets and clothing, to the children of war-torn Sarajevo as well as assisting in Operation Christmas Child, overseeing the delivery of toys and presents from UK schoolchildren to children in Bosnia.

Helping Others

Apart from 1984's high-profiled *We Are The World* charity single, Michael has always been deeply committed to helping those less fortunate than himself. As Steven Spielberg writes in the sleeve notes for *HIStory*, Heal The World "works to preserve this planet's most precious resources - children, and the environment." Through the foundation, Michael has helped countless numbers around the world, improving their quality of life and spreading a little happiness. He is also well known for performing at charity events and giving concerts, the profits from which all go to charity. One example of this was the 'Michael Jackson & Friends - What More Can I Give' charity concerts in June 1999 that were organised by Michael in conjunction with the Red Cross. At performances in Seoul and Munich, Jackson was joined by a host of artists including, All Saints, Mariah Carey, Luther Vandross, Boyzone, Ringo Starr and Boyz II Men. Ticket sales and a TV 'Telethon' raised close to 3 million dollars which went to the Red Cross, UNESCO and the Nelson Mandela Children's Fund. In addition to these well publicised, high profile events, Jackson is also involved with countless small acts of kindness every year. From sending money to help sick children with their medical care, to opening up his Neverland Ranch to disabled and disadvantaged children, Michael is one of the most generous people in the music business. In fact he was even listed in the year 2000 edition of the *Guinness Book Of Records* as having broken the record for the 'Most Charities Supported By A Pop Star'. Some of these are as follows:

AIDS Project L.A.	Congressional Black Caucus (CBC)	Society of Singers
American Cancer Society	Dakar Foundation	Starlight Foundation
Angel Food	Dreamstreet Kids	The Carter Center's Atlanta Project
Big Brothers of Greater Los Angeles	Dreams Come True Charity	The Sickle Cell Research Foundation
BMI Foundation, Inc.	Elizabeth Taylor Aids Foundation	Transafrica
Brotherhood Crusade	Juvenile Diabetes Foundation	United Negro College Fund (UNCF)
Brothman Burn Center	Love Match	United Negro College Fund Ladder's
Camp Ronald McDonald	Make-A-Wish Foundation	of Hope
Childhelp U.S.A.	Minority Aids Project	Volunteers of America
Children's Institute International	Motown Museum	Watts Summer Festival
Cities and Schools Scholarship Fund	NAACP	Wish Granting
Community Youth Sports & Arts	National Rainbow Coalition	YMCA - 28th Street/Crenshaw
Foundation	Rotary Club of Australia	

NAME: MICHAEL JACKSON

DOB: AUGUST 25, 1958

PLACE OF BIRTH: GARY, INDIANA

JACKSON ACCUSED

Perhaps the most devastating event in Jackson's life was the child abuse scandal of the early 1990's. On the 17th of August 1993, police in LA were informed about an allegation that Michael had sexually molested a thirteen-year-old boy. It took five days for the story to leak out to the media, and within 24 hours the story had gone round the world like wild fire. With the press hungry for information, a copy of the case report containing the full lurid details of the allegations was leaked from the LA Department Of Children's Services. These were widely reported at the time as were the 'inside' stories of anyone connected with Jackson. With large sums of money on offer, former employees came out of the wood work attesting to what they may have seen. Nevertheless, when these stories were later checked out by the LAPD, they were found to be groundless. Similarly, the police questioned more than thirty children and their families but, despite stringent examination, could not find anyone to support the case against Michael.

While the Californian authorities were investigating the criminal allegations against Jackson, the boy's family launched a civil lawsuit, claiming 30 million dollars in damages. Jackson's side issued a counter claim for extortion and were confidently gearing up to fight the civil court case when it was announced on November 12th that Michael was cancelling his world tour and entering a rehab programme to cure an addiction to painkillers. Due to his emotional fragility at this time and the toil that a lengthy court case with all the attendant press coverage would have on him, it was decided to settle out of court. It has also been speculated that political and racial issues could have gone against Jackson and that neither legal team really wanted the stigma of losing the case.

Consequently, at the end of January 1994, Jackson agreed to pay the boy an undisclosed sum while in turn he withdrew his extortion charges. In a statement after the settlement his attorney said, "The resolution of this case is in no way an admission of guilt by Michael Jackson. In short, he is an innocent man who does not intend to have his career and his life destroyed by rumour and innuendo". Later, in September 1994, the Los Angeles and Santa Barbara County District Attorneys issued a statement which said that despite exhaustive enquires that lasted over a year and the interview of 400 witnesses, no charges were to be brought against Michael.

Although that was the end of the initial legal fallout from the charges, and despite assertions that he was innocent, Jackson has had a hard time recovering his public persona. It has to be remembered that Michael was never arrested or charged with any crime, but this fact is not widely appreciated by the general public. Those that know him best, his close friends and family, stood by him throughout. Elton John let Michael hide out in secret in his home at the end of 1993 when he was fighting his addiction to painkillers, while the likes of Elizabeth Taylor, Macauley Culkin and Bruce Willis issued statements in his support.

However, that was not the end of the affair. In 1995 a journalist called Victor Gutierrez claimed on the US TV show *Hard Copy* that he knew of a video tape containing footage of Michael Jackson molesting a boy. Despite assertions to the contrary in the programme, the LAPD stated clearly that they were not re-opening the investigation. Jackson issued a massive slander suit against Gutierrez and *Hard Copy* but no one could produce a copy of the video nor corroborate Gutierrez's story. On October 15th 1996, the judge ruled that the story was malicious and untrue, and Gutierrez was responsible for damages. Despite fleeing to Mexico and declaring himself bankrupt, in April 1998, he was ordered to pay out almost three million dollars in damages to Jackson.

Despite the continuing career accolades, Michael was becoming a more reclusive figure. This only succeeded in increasing his enigmatic status as he was spending more of his time seeking the domestic happiness he so craved. Indeed, he was to give his first television interview in years to American chat show queen Oprah Winfrey in which he openly talked about himself, his music and his hopes for the future. His superstar status was evident as the 90-minute interview, broadcast live around the world, was to become the fourth most-watched event in television history.

His relentless pursuit of personal happiness, though, was to see his first marriage sadly break down. Michael had married Lisa-Marie Presley, the daughter of Elvis Presley, in May 1994, sparking a tabloid frenzy as they became one of the most sought after couples amongst the celebrity-hungry media. The marriage fell apart less than two years later and the couple quickly divorced. In the midst of all this activity in his personal life, Michael returned to the musical coalface with a double album, containing new music as well as a collection of remixed old hits, that was released in June 1995. The fans were delighted and, after some years of media scrutiny, those close to Michael were pleased to see him concentrate on what he does best - making music.

Lisa Marie Presley

Lisa Marie Presley is the only child of Elvis and Priscilla Presley. Her and Michael first met in 1974 backstage at a Jackson Five concert which she had been taken to by her father. Due to the fact that Michael was 16 and Lisa Marie was 6, they had little in common at the time, but continued to see each other sporadically at various music events. When she was 20 years old, Lisa married musician Danny Keough and had two children but sadly after 6 years it ended in divorce. Towards the end of her marriage, once she had separated from Danny, Lisa and Michael became firm friends and started dating. Within three weeks of her divorce, on May 26th 1994, Lisa and Michael were married at La Vega in the Dominican Republic.

As with most things in Michael's life, controversy was not far behind. The tabloid press had a field day and claimed that the marriage had been arranged to dispel rumours that Jackson had molested children. Likewise, it was also rumoured that Lisa was trying to get her singing career off the ground. Despite this, both asserted that they were in love and it was not a marriage of convenience. Sadly though, their relationship was not to last and they filed for divorce in January 1996 citing "irreconcilable differences". Since their separation, Lisa has been romantically involved with Luke Watson (a friend of her first husband), musician John Oszajca and the actor Nicholas Cage.

CHAPTER 11

MICHAEL JACKSON
HEALING THE WORLD

HEALING THE WORLD

The next entry in Michael's discography was to be the part-retrospective *HIStory: Past, Present And Future Book 1*. The 2-CD set was aptly-titled, as the album combines one disc of songs that helped to secure his position as King of Pop, providing us with an irresistible greatest hits collection, whilst the second brings us the new Michael Jackson.

Jarvis And Jackson

During Jackson's performance of 'Earth Song' at the 1996 Brit Awards, Jarvis Cocker, lead singer of the British band Pulp, invaded the stage. Cocker had become increasingly annoyed by what he saw as Michael's quasi-religious pretensions. He also thought that it was distasteful for Jackson to feature child performers in his act given the recent child abuse scandal. The invasion was more comic than threatening with Cocker wiggling his backside at the audience, waving his arms and lifting his cardigan up as he was chased across the stage by Jackson's minders. After the performance Jackson's team alleged that he had trodden on a child dancer in the fracas and the police were involved. Cocker was questioned first in his dressing room and then at a local police station before being released without charge in the early hours of the morning. By this time the story was plastered all over the front pages of the world's press and the resultant publicity led to soaring sales of Pulp's album *Different Class* and Michael's single *Earth Song*.

The more recent material saw him in biting form, imbuing his music with a new-found aggression, most notably on the single *They Don't Care About Us* and album track 'Money'. The album of new tunes was his strongest and most musically varied in years, containing what many believe to be one of his finest ever compositions, 'Stranger in Moscow'.

Considering Michael's well-documented humanitarian character, it was not surprising that the record, like his previous album *Dangerous*, contained another smash-hit created directly from his political conscience. *Earth Song* was a successful attempt at challenging the big issues close to Michael's heart: war and pollution and went to number one in Britain.

The rest of *HIStory* is mouth-watering and it went on to do what most Michael Jackson albums do best - break records. The first single, *Scream*, a duet with his sister Janet, was accompanied by an award-winning video, on which both Jacksons appeared. The video

cost an astonishing $7 million to produce, breaking the record Michael had previously set for *Thriller* as the most expensive music video ever made. The single broke another record by entering the *Billboard* Hot 100 Singles Chart at number five, smashing the 25-year old position held by The Beatles for their single *Let It Be*, which entered at number six in 1970. The video itself went on to win a host of MTV awards including those for Best Dance Video, Best Choreography and Best Art Direction. Amazingly, Michael was to break his own record when another single from the album, *You Are Not Alone* became the first single in history to enter the *Billboard* Charts at number one. The record-breaking didn't end there, though. Such was the faith Sony Music had in Michael Jackson, that they were prepared to spend an unprecedented $30 million in promoting the album world-wide.

HIStory (1995)

Total sales exceeded 15 million. It debuted at number 1 on the Billboard Album Chart where it remained for 2 weeks. It also went to number 1 in the UK Album Charts.

Highest UK Single Chart Positions	Highest US Single Chart Positions
1 You Are Not Alone	1 You Are Not Alone
1 Earth Song	5 Scream
3 Scream / Childhood	5 Childhood
4 They Don't Care About Us	30 They Don't Care About Us
4 Stranger In Moscow	

This included creating 20-foot high statues of the King of Pop across five continents, the British version being towed down the River Thames via tugboat, allowing his UK contingent of fans to witness an extraordinary promotional event.

Sony's belief in the continuing commercial prosperity of their leading asset was well rewarded, with the album selling 15 million copies across the world, being certified 5 times platinum within two months of release, and the accompanying world tour being attended by more than 4 1/2 million people.

Many of the album's tracks were remixed and remastered for a new audience in the more dance-orientated release *Blood On The Dance Floor: HIStory In The Mix*, which featured some of the top names in dance music such as Todd Terry and David Morales. 'Earth Song' was transformed into a resonant piece of trance music with it's atmospheric remix, whilst 'You Are Not Alone' is brought into the age of house music with it's lush, loungey beat and deftly-delivered lyrics.

Indeed, Michael was becoming something of a workaholic and he returned to the world of film, producing and starring in the mini-feature *Ghosts*, which was premiered at the 1997 Cannes Film Festival. The movie is a slight return to *Thriller* territory with its heavy reliance upon the supernatural. Michael undertakes five different roles - as Maestro, Mayor, Ghoul Mayor, Superghoul and Skeleton - in a film designed to appeal to the child in all of us, utilising extensive special effects.

In the midst of this punishing work schedule, he surprised many by marrying the woman who would become the mother of his children. It had already been announced that Michael was to become a father and in November 1996, and ten months after his divorce from Lisa-Marie Presley, Michael married Deborah Rowe, a long-standing friend, in Sydney, Australia. The birth of his son followed in February 1997 and he was named Prince Michael Junior, after Michael's grandfather. The Jackson family unit was completed in April 1998 when Deborah gave birth to a second child, a daughter, exotically named Paris. Sadly, the marriage did not last, with the couple filing for divorce in October 1999, but a press statement was issued in which they made clear their intention to remain friends. Michael has gone on record stating that he finds parenthood blissful and describes his children as his dream come true. After more than 25 years of making music fans very happy indeed, Michael Jackson has now discovered his own happiness in becoming a father. The world could only sit back and applaud.

Blood On The Dance Floor (1997)
Total sales were just under 4 million.
It went to number 16 on the Billboard Album Charts and number 1 on the UK Album Charts, where it remained for two weeks.

Highest UK Single Chart Positions
1 Blood on the Dance Floor
5 HIStory (Remix) / Ghosts
Highest US Single Chart Positions
42 Blood On The Dance Floor

Michael and Debbie

Like his previous marriage to Lisa Marie, Michael's relationship with Debbie has also been plagued by controversy. The press pretty much decided early on that it was a further attempt to prove Michael's normality. In November 1996 a UK tabloid paper said that Debbie had conceived a child through artificial insemination and was being paid to have Jackson's baby. This created a rush of media speculation that put both their lives under the spotlight. At the beginning of 1997 they declared in a joint statement that: 'Deborah is adamant about again setting the record straight that Michael is the father of the child, the pregnancy is not the result of artificial means, that she has not been paid to have Michael's baby, and that she is not seeking or filing for a divorce".

However, despite these earlier assurances, and following the birth of their two children, on the 8th October 1999 they did file for divorce.

MICHAEL JACKSON
THE BEAT GOES ON

THE BEAT GOES ON

On September 7th and September 10th 2001, Michael held two very special concerts a Madison Square Garden in New York City to celebrate 30 years as a solo artist. In addition to the thirty-five thousand people who were lucky (or rich) enough to see Jackson play live, the concerts were broadcast as a CBS special on November 13th drawing an estimated 45 million viewers. This show was also screened later on TV around the globe meaning an estimated 110 million people saw it.

Invincible (2001)
This debuted at number 1 on the Billboard Album Charts where it remained for 14 weeks, while in the UK it reached number 3.

Highest UK Single Chart Positions
2 You Rock My World
25 Cry
Highest US Single Chart Positions
10 You Rock My World

A veritable who's who of showbiz and music came along and paid tribute to Michael over these two nights Amongst others, those who performed included Mya, Usher, Whitney Houston, Gladys Knight, Ricky Martin, Luther Vandross, Dionne Warwick, Shaggy, Jill Scott, Monica Gloria Estefan, Liza Minelli, Destiny's Child, Ray Charles, 'N Sync and Britney Spears. With typical Jackson excess, the show featured a forty-eigh piece orchestra, twelve background singers, a three-hundred member gospel choir, a two-hundred member children's choir, and a forty member dance ensemble. The highlight was a reunion of The Jackson Five who played through many of their old hits such as 'ABC', 'The Love You Save' and 'I'll Be There'. Jackson fans were also enthralled with solo hits such as 'The Way You Make Me Feel', 'Billie Jean', 'Beat It' and 'You Rock My World while the whole show wound up with a special performance of 'We Are the World' ir which everyone present joined in.

One other highlight from this concert was Jackson's showcasing of material from his new album *Invincible*, probably the most critically important release of Jackson's career Executive produced by Michael himself, with contributions from the world's top production and songwriting talent, it was his first studio album for six years. Taking more than a year to record, mainly at studios in New York and Los Angeles and costing more than 20 million dollars, Michael put down more than thirty songs which were late whittled down to the final 16 that are on the album. Any worries about how well it was going to do were quashed soon after release at the end of October 2001 as it went straight in at number 1 in the USA, Australia and much of Europe.

The first single off the new album, *You Rock My World*, which was written and produced by Michael and Rodney Jerkins, premiered on the Michael Jackson official web-site on August 24th before going out to radio stations. Officially released on October 8th 2001, the single was also accompanied by a spectacular video that premiered in late September 2001. This was directed by Paul Hunter and starred Michael with Marlon Brando, Chris Tucker and Michael Madson. The full version was a *Thriller*esque 14 minutes long, however a shorter 5 minute version was also produced that tends to be shown more often on music video channels such as MTV. This single became the 28th top ten solo hit for Michael Jackson reaching number 10 in the Billboard Hot 100 singles chart. It also went straight in at number 2 in the UK chart and number 4 in Australia.

The next single *Cry*, which was produced by Michael Jackson and R. Kelly, was released first via Michael's official web site on September 20, 2001. Following a commercial single release on December 3rd 2001, it has steadily climbed charts across the globe. The video for this single was directed by Nick Brandt, who previously worked with Michael on the videos for 'Earthsong', 'Childhood' and 'Stranger In Moscow', although Michael does not appear in it.

As with the African famine in the first half of the 1980's, more than 15 years later, Michael led the drive to release another charity single, although this time the recipients were much closer to home. The morning after his Madison Square Garden concert on the 10th of September 2001, the American way of life was permanently altered. It is perhaps not surprising that Michael reacted in the way he knows best. With contributions from over thirty individuals and groups including 'N Sync, Ricky Martin, Mariah Carey, Carlos Santana, Celine Dion, Tom Petty, Julio Iglesias, Reba McEntire, Beyoncé Knowles, Hanson, Gloria Estefan and Ziggy Marley, the song *What More Can I Give* was released in November 2001. Michael performed the song at a fund-raising concert at the RFK Stadium in Washington, DC on October 21st 2001, emphasising that, "This is dedicated to being an American, each and every one of you, and everyone we lost September 11th". With high hopes to raise many millions for the victims' families, Michael showed once again that he feels very deeply for people less fortunate than himself.

Invincible **involves the talents of:**
Walter Afanasieff, Robin Thicke, Carole Bayer Sager, Boyz II Men, DeVante, Emilio Estefan, Jr., Fats, David Foster, Dave "Jam" Hall, Rodney Jerkins, R. Kelly, Missy Elliott, Warren Riker, Carlos Santana, Sisqo, Will Smith and Bruce Swedien.

CHAPTER 13

MICHAEL JACKSON
DREAMS COME TRUE

CHAPTER THIRTEEN
DREAMS CAN COME TRUE

The music press are always keen to put labels on our pop stars, such as The Boss for Bruce Springsteen or The Guv'nor for Bob Dylan, but only the very best earn royalty status. From the King of Rock 'n' Roll himself, Elvis Presley, through Solomon Burke, labelled the King of Soul, we now have the King of Pop. For his outstanding contribution to pop music, Michael Jackson was inducted into the Rock 'n' Roll Hall of Fame in March 2001. The ceremony was held at the plush Waldorf Astoria Hotel in New York City and was a celebration of Michael's life and work; an opportunity for the music industry to pay tribute to the man. Michael had already been inducted into the fabled Hall of Fame with The Jackson 5, and was now becoming the youngest-ever solo artist to achieve the same reward.

As we have learned, though, this is far from the only unprecedented achievement Michael has acquired during his astonishing career. He has the longest succession of number one hits in the United States. He shares the record for the most Grammy awards won in a single year. He holds the record for an album going to the top spot in more countries than any other musician in history, as well as having the distinction of producing the most number one singles from a solitary album. Oh, and there's the small matter of co-writing one of the best-selling singles of all time with *We Are The World*.

Whatever the future might hold for Michael Jackson, he can be assured that the past belongs to him. During the course of his career, he has changed the music business forever, bringing us a fine blend of pop, soul and disco as well as crossing the race divide by breaking down barriers between black and white music. He is an artist who stole hearts when leading The Jackson 5 and then delivered knockout punches as a record-busting solo performer. His music has broken hearts, healed hearts and has sound-tracked the lives of an entire generation. He is the one, the only King of Pop - Michael Joseph Jackson.

Michael's first TV appearance was in August 1969 during the *Miss Black America Pageant*.

Michael made his first appearance on *American Bandstand* in September 1972.

In the late 1980's, Michael attempted to buy the skeleton of 'The Elephant Man', John Merrick, from the London hospital that owned it.

The grounds of Michael's Neverland Ranch also contain his own private zoo.

Michael suffered second degree burns while filming a Pepsi commercial, after a visual effect went wrong.

On occasions, Michael has used look alikes to avoid the crowds that always flock to every public appearance.

Michael's autobiography *Moonwalk* is dedicated to Fred Astaire.

The Jackson's first Motown single release *I Want You Back* sold two million copies in six weeks.

Michael was apprehended by police in the USA while shopping at a jewellers in Los Angeles in disguise.

Pepsi ended their relationship with Michael during the child abuse scandal creating outrage amongst his fans.

Michael first appeared on the cover of *Rolling Stone* magazine in April 1971.

Michael's favourite piece of music is *Prélude à l'Après-Midi d'un Faune* by the French classical composer Debussy.

Michelangelo is the historical individual that Michael would most like to meet.

Michael suffered a great deal from acne when he was a teenager.

In 1993, Michael was crowned honorary King of a province in Ghana, Africa. He is also an honorary member of the Bafokeng Ka Bakwena tribe in Phokeng, Africa.

In April 1997, as part of the promotion for *Blood On The Dance Floor*, Jackson's record company shipped safes containing a copy of the single to DJ's. These all had to be opened at a designated time and prevented anyone from hearing the record before they were supposed to.

The *Making Of Michael Jackson's Thriller*, released in 1983, is one of the largest-selling music home-videos ever, with more than 900,000 units sold.

The original album cover for *Ben* showed a group of rats superimposed on a picture of Michael and was withdrawn soon after release due to the distress to younger fans. It was reissued without any rats.

Some of Michael's less talented brothers nicknamed him 'Big Nose'. This teasing led him to have plastic surgery on his nose.

Although *Thriller* is the biggest selling album by Michael, many commentators consider *Off The Wall* to be his best.

The short film for *Bad* was directed by the famous Hollywood director Martin Scorsese.

At the post-*Thriller* Grammy Award ceremony, the host Mickey Rooney said, "It's a pleasure doing The Michael Jackson Show."

Michael first picked up the title 'King Of Pop' following meteoric sales of his album *Bad*.

President Bush senior proclaimed Michael Jackson 'Artist of the Decade' in a White House Ceremony at the end of the 1980's.

Michael sold in excess of 110 million records in the 1980's.

MICHAEL JACKSON

Michael is said to have recorded 70 songs for *Dangerous* before choosing the final 14 that would appear on the album.

'Will You Be There' from *Dangerous* opens with an extract of Beethoven's 9th Symphony as performed by the Cleveland Orchestra. Sadly no-one had asked their permission and it resulted in a 7 million dollar law suit that Sony settled out of court.

The tune for 'Smile' on *History* was written by Charlie Chaplin.

In 1988, Michael's autobiography *Moonwalk* topped the best seller lists in both the USA and UK.

If you combine Jackson's solo work with his earlier Motown and Epic releases, he has sold more than 240 million records around the globe.

Michael performed from a wheelchair at the 1993 Soul Train Music Awards after injuring his ankle.

Michael often writes notes that he throws from his hotel room window to fans waiting below.

Macaulay Culkin is Godfather to both of Michael's children.

A sculpture of 'Michael Jackson and Bubbles' by artist Jeff Koons sold at an auction in 2001 for US $5,615,750.

Monopoly is Michael's favourite board game.

Michael's favourite animals at the Neverland Ranch - Jeannine the Ostrich, Muscles the Snake, Bubbles the Chimp, Louie the Llama, Suzie the Rabbit, Uncle Tookie the Frog and Spanky the Dog - can also be bought as limited edition toys.

Michael once owned a cement garden statue of Narcissus, the ancient Greek hero who fell in love with his own reflection. Showing his sense of humour, he named it 'Michael'.

Michael is Godfather to 'Bee-Gee' Barry Gibb's son Michael.

Michael has endorsed products including soft drinks, chocolate bars, scarves, T-shirts and dolls. His face has even appeared on postage stamps.

Michael has never taken any formal dancing lessons.

The Hard Rock Cafe chain have virtually made an industry of buying up Michael Jackson memorabilia.

Michael has a high-school diploma.

Michael's friend Princess Stephanie of Monaco is the mystery girl in the song 'In The Closet'.

Michael has used fragments of classical music by Beethoven, Mussorgsky and Orff in his songs.

At the American Music Awards in 2002, Michael received the 'Artist Of The Century' award.

Michael has never purchased or even slept in an oxygen chamber.

La Toya is the only other member of the Jackson family who suffers from vitiligo.

Michael and his brothers gave their mother a £75,000 Rolls Royce for her 56th birthday.

Michael is a huge fan of Walt Disney with Mickey Mouse, Pinocchio and (of course) Peter Pan being amongst his favourite cartoon characters.

The first record that Michael ever bought was *Mickey's Monkey* by Smokey Robinson and the Miracles.

Michael intends to establish a school at the Neverland Ranch which his children, Prince and Paris, can attend.

Michael hates to do any exercise other than dancing.

Michael is a vegetarian.

The Michael Jackson brand is as recognised across the globe as Coca Cola.

Contrary to tabloid stories, Michael is not going to be frozen when he dies so that his body can be revived in the future.

Michael has a selection of golf buggies which he uses to travel around the Neverland Ranch.

If he could be any superhero, Michael has stated he would like to be Morph from the X-Men.

Michael almost featured in the Steven Spielberg *Peter Pan* film.

Quincy Jones nicknamed Jackson 'Smelly' when the singer stopped taking showers while recording *Off The Wall*.

Billie Jean was the first video by a black artist to be added to MTV's regular playlist.

Tatum O'Neal was Michael's first date.

Michael and Elizabeth Taylor both deny that he ever proposed marriage.

Bubbles was rescued by Michael from a cancer-research laboratory in Texas.

A young French fan committed suicide in 1984, after his parents refused to pay for plastic surgery to make him look like Michael Jackson.

In 1986 Michael was let off overdue library fines on the condition that he returned the books autographed.

Michael has a star on the Hollywood Boulevard, outside Mann's Chinese Theatre.

You can write to Michael Jackson at Neverland Valley Ranch, co/ Postmaster, Los Olivos, CA 93441, USA.

Michael's appearance at the 35th Grammy Awards in 1993, at which he was honored with a Living Legend Award, was watched by 1.2 Billion people across the globe.

Peter Pan is one of Michael's favourite books.

Michael has done commercials for Suzuki and Pepsi.

When Michael appeared on the NBC programme *Motown 25: Yesterday, Today, Forever*, his Moonwalk was watched by almost 50 million viewers.

Jackson's interview with Oprah Winfrey on the 10th of February 1993 was seen by more than 100 million viewers.

The 1982 storybook album for *E.T. - The Extra Terrestrial*, won Michael a Grammy for Best Children's Recording

Thriller is the most popular album of all time in the USA.

Michael is 5'10" or 178 cm tall.

In February 2001, Michael gave a speech at the Oxford University Union on child welfare.

Michael appeared in *The Simpsons* in 1991 but was not permitted to sing by his record company. Instead, the songs were performed by a Jackson imitator.

Ronald Reagan presented Michael with a special presidential award in 1984 for setting an outstanding example to youth.

The Jackson's were the first pop act to have four consecutive number one singles.

Since 1994, Michael has had his own record company, MJJ music. He has released records by 3T (his nephews Ttaj, Taryll and T.J.) as well as work by his older sister Rebbie.

101 FACTS ABOUT

Jackson has his own music publishing company called Mijac music.

Quincy Jones thought seriously about renaming *Billy Jean* in case listeners thought Michael was singing about the tennis player Billy Jean King.

On Good Friday 1985, *We Are The World* was broadcast at a designated time by almost 9,000 radio stations across the globe.

Michael cannot read or write music.

133 million viewers watched Michael's half-time performance of songs from *Dangerous* during the 1993 Super Bowl.

Prior to the release of *Dangerous*, 30,000 copies were stolen from Los Angeles airport in an armed robbery.

Michael can play several musical instruments including keyboards, drums, bass, percussion and guitar.

One in twelve people in the UK own a copy of *Bad*.

Jackson's *Dangerous* album spawned seven Top Ten hits, a UK record.

HIStory: Past, Present, and Future - Book 1 is the best selling double album of all time in the UK.

In the UK, *Blood on the Dance Floor* is the best selling single artist remix album ever.

Earth Song was Michael Jackson's best ever selling UK single with more than a million sold.

Michael carried the coffin at Sammy Davis Jr.'s funeral along with Bill Cosby, Frank Sinatra and Dean Martin.

Thriller won Michael seven American Music Awards, eight Grammy Awards, four American Video Awards and three MTV Video Awards.

Thriller sold more than a million copies in December 1982.

Guitar Hero Eddie Van Halen played the guitar solo on *Beat It* and still plays live with Jackson.

Before the Jacksons made it big they used to live at 2300 Jackson Street. The Jackson whom the street was named after was not a relation.

Michael is in fact one of the ten Jackson children. However, Marlon's twin brother died in infancy.

Marvin Gaye and Stevie Wonder were Michael's childhood friends, they used to come to his house and play with him and the other Jackson siblings.

In November 1970 threats made on Michael's life by teenage gangs led to the cancellation of a concert in Buffalo, New York.

Michael is still as great as ever!

MICHAEL JACKSON

"Because with time my skin condition has gotten worse. I have vitiligo and I'm totally completely allergic to the sun. I'm not even supposed to be outside actually. Even if I'm in the shade the sun rays can destroy my skin"

"I feel guilty having to put my name, sometimes, on the songs that I - I do write them, I compose them, I do the scoring, I do the lyrics, I do the melodies, but still, it's a... It's a work of God."

"I think a great artist should be able to just create any style, any form, anything from rock to pop to folk to gospel to spiritual...from the Irish farmer to a lady who scrubs toilets in Harlem."

"I always know what's going on, on the radio and in clubs, that people are listening to. Even though people think I live at Neverland - mentally I'm in Never Never Land all the time - I'm always connected."

"I don't want to scare people to the point where they're afraid to go to sleep."

"I've had musicians who really get angry with me because I'll make them do something literally several hundred to a thousand times till it's what I want it to be."

"My favorite thing is to climb trees, go all the way up to the top of a tree and I look down on the branches. Whenever I do that it inspires me for music."

"It's being offstage that's difficult for me."

"I've met Britney several times and she was very sweet and humble. She came to my room. We quietly talked for couple of hours and she was just, uh, like a Barbie doll."

"I don't create the dance, the dance creates itself, really."

"Even if you're sweeping floors or painting ceilings, do it better than anybody in the world."

"I would love to see a celebration for children. Children's Day; a holiday. We have Mother's Day, Father's Day - no Children's Day."

"I love dressing up like some kind of monster or something and knocking on the doors. Nobody knows it's me and I get candy." Michael on Halloween

"My dream was to make something with a beginning, a middle and an ending, like a short film." Michael on *Thriller*

"If I don't get exactly what I'm looking for, I get very depressed."

"Songwriting is a very frustrating art form."

"I like to study people - be like the fly on the wall."

"I don't find my interest in animals weird or strange at all."

"All of Hollywood has plastic surgery! I don't know why they [the press] point me out. It's just to my nose, you know."

"I'm surprised she loves dolls. My sister Janet didn't like that sort of thing. She was a tomboy." Michael on his daughter Paris

"I told my father I'm going to match his record." Michael on having more children.

"If it weren't for my desire to help the children of the world, I'd throw in the towel and kill myself."

"I wrote a song called Dirty Diana. It was not about Lady Diana. It was about a certain kind of girls that hang around concerts or clubs... You know, they call them groupies."

"In my heart, I was saying, "I love you, Diana. Shine. And shine on forever ... because you are the true princess of the people." And in words, I did not say it ..." Michael on Princess Diana

"I go around the world dealing with running and hiding. I can't take a walk in the park... I can't go to the store... I have to hide in the room. You feel like in prison."

"I grew up in a fishbowl. I will not allow that to happen to my son."

"Michael originally rang me up on Christmas day...and I didn't believe it was him. I didn't think it was Michael...eventually I said, 'Is that really you?' He was laughing on the phone, he said, 'You don't believe me do you?'" **Paul McCartney** on the first time Michael proposed they work together.

"He had a real intensity...People take him for a simpleton with a head full of silly songs, but he's a complex young man, curious about everything, who wants to go further and further. He behaves like an adolescent and, at the same time, like a wise old philosopher. **Quincy Jones**

"It was a child's dream, with every kind of soda in the world there, every kind of candy. A two-floor arcade, a carnival and a movie theatre." **Macaulay Culkin** describing Neverland.

"Michael never really had a childhood and I think he is trying to experience it in later life. I would tell him to keep the knowledge that he is innocent and hold his head up." **Frank Dileo**, Michael's former manager.

"You can't say somebody's guilty of a crime when you have no evidence to prove it...I hate the media for what they do to Michael, I do hate them." **Whitney Houston**

"When I met him, it was really love at first sight. I think when you get to know Michael, you understand the nature of his charisma... He looks at the world with the innocent eyes of a child." **Sophia Loren**

"My manager came to me and asked me if I wanted to work with Michael...I thought about it for less than a second." **R. Kelly**

"When Michael Jackson sings, it is with the voice of angels, and when his feet move, you can see God dancing." **Sir Bob Geldof**

"Michael would rather cut his wrist than harm a child." **Liz Taylor**

"You want to see the boy next door?...(then) don't go see Michael Jackson, because he ain't the boy next door." **Sammy Davis, Jr.**

"He is the greatest...If I tried to compare him to, say Gene Kelly or even Fred Astaire, I would do him an injustice, because the thing that makes him great is his own style and his own originality." **Hermes Pan**, Fred Astaire's choreographer.

"We had very similar experiences in childhood. We're both going to be eight years old forever in some place because we never had a chance to be eight when we actually were." **Macaulay Culkin**

"Michael can go out and perform before 90,000 people, but if I ask him to sing a song for me, I have to sit on the couch with my hands over my eyes and he goes behind the couch. He is amazingly shy." **Quincy Jones**

"I think Michael appeals to the child in all of us, he has the quality of innocence that we would all like to obtain or have kept. ...I think he is one of the finest people to hit this planet, and, in my estimation, he is the true King of Pop, Rock and Soul. I love you Michael." **Elizabeth Taylor**

"It's an incredible project to even be a part of. I'm blessed to even be in the position to work with the greatest entertainer of all time. Just to be working with him is a phenomenon itself, you know, a dream come true..." **Rodney Jerkins** on working with Jackson on *Invincible*.

"He never had a childhood. He is having one now. His buddies are 12-year-old kids. They have pillow fights and food fights." **Bert Fields**, a former attorney of Jackson's.

"My friendship with him is the most important thing to me, and if this marriage gets in the way of that friendship, then we'll put that marriage aside." **Debbie Rowe**

"I would never do this for money, I did this because I love him. That's the only reason I did this." **Debbie Rowe**

TOUROGRAPHY

THE JACKSON 5

The Jackson 5 First National Tour - Fall 1970
The Jackson 5 began their first-ever tour on October 9th 1970. The tour stopped in multiple US states and cities, including Boston, Cincinnati, and New York City, breaking venue attendance records at several stops.

The Jackson 5 US Tour - Summer 1971
This took in 40 dates at a range of US cities, including Philadelphia, New York, and Milwaukee.

The Jackson 5 US Tour - Late 1971
Appearances at venues in 50 US cities.

The Jackson 5 European Tour - November 1972
This 12-day tour of Europe saw them greeted by screaming crowds at Heathrow airport and a sell out gig at the Liverpool Empire, breaking the venues attendance record that had previously been held by The Beatles.

The Jackson 5 World Tour - March 1973 to February 1975
This mammoth touring effort was undertaken to capitalise on their growing global success. Starting in the USA, they went to Japan, Hawaii, Africa, the United Kingdom, South America, Japan, Hong Kong, Australia, New Zealand, the Philippines and the West Indies. Undertaken over almost two years, they often returned to the USA for rest and recreation and to play further concerts in their home country.

THE JACKSONS

European Tour - May 1977
The Jacksons spent two and a half weeks touring France, Germany, Holland and the UK where they also performed at a Royal Command Performance for the Queen of England.

Interim Tour - January 1978
Tour of the USA and Europe.

The Destiny World Tour - from January 1979
To promote their new album *Destiny*, The Jacksons toured 80 US cities as well as playing numerous dates in France, Holland, Switzerland, Kenya and the UK. Several concerts had to be cancelled due to Michael catching a flu.

The Triumph Tour - 1981
In 1981, The Jacksons embarked on one of their most successful tours ever, a 36-city trek that grossed $5.5 million. Beginning in Memphis, Tennessee, and concluding with 4 sold out shows in Los Angeles, it has been described by *Rolling Stone* magazine as one of the greatest live shows of the 1970's and 80's.

The Victory Tour - July to December, 1984
This tour of the US and Canada was Michael Jackson's last as lead singer of The Jacksons. Spanning 55 dates over 5 months, more than two million people came to see the group. The tour earned in excess of 75 million dollars, although Michael donated all of his earnings to charity.

MICHAEL'S SOLO TOURS

The Bad World Tour - September 12, 1987 to January 27, 1989

The first of Michael's solo tours, this started out in Tokyo on September 12, 1987, and concluded in Los Angeles on January 27, 1989. During these 16 months, Michael visited 15 countries and performed to more than four million people, grossing over 125 million dollars. Officially the biggest and highest earning tour of all time, Jackson's seven sold out shows at Wembley Stadium attracted more than half a million people, setting a new World record.

The Dangerous World Tour - June 27, 1992 - November 11, 1993

This tour was front page news everywhere it went. With extravagant staging that took almost three days to set up and 20 trucks of equipment shuttled between countries on Cargo planes, almost 3.5 million fans flocked to see Jackson at 69 concert dates. Starting at Munich's Olympic Stadium on June 27th, and ending in Mexico City on November 11th, amongst other places Michael performed in Japan, Asia, Russia, Turkey, Israel, Mexico, and South America, donating all the proceeds to his Heal The World Foundation and other charities. Sadly the tour was cut short due to illness.

The HIStory World Tour - September 7, 1996 - October 15, 1997

The HIStory World Tour began in Prague, Czech Republic on September 7, 1996 and ended in Durban, South Africa on October 15, 1997. At the conclusion of the tour, Michael had played at 82 concerts to a total of over 4.5 million fans in 58 cities, 35 countries, and 5 continents, with an average concert attendance of 54,878.

MICHAEL JACKSON DISCOGRAPHY

SOLO ALBUMS

Got To Be There *Ain't No Sunshine / I Wanna Be Where You Are / Girl Don't Take Your Love From Me / In Our Small Way / Got To Be There / Rockin' Robin / Wings Of My Love / Maria (You Were The Only One) / Love Is Here And Now You're Gone / You've Got A Friend*
LP - Motown 1972 (CD Reissue - WD 1989)

Ben *Ben / Greatest Show On Earth / People Make The World Go 'Round / We've Got A Good Thing Going / Everybody's Somebody's Fool / My Girl / What Goes Around Comes Around / In Our Small Way / Shoo-Be-Doo-Be-Doo-Da-Day / You Can Cry On My Shoulder*
LP - Motown 1972 (CD Reissue - WD 1989)

Forever, Michael *We're Almost There / Take Me Back / One Day In Your Life / Cinderella / Stay Awhile / We've Got Forever / Just A Little Bit Of You / You Are There / Dapper Dan / Dear Michael / I'll Come Home To You*
LP - Motown 1975 (CD Reissue - WD 1990)

Off The Wall *Don't Stop 'Til You Get Enough / Rock With You / Working Day And Night / Get On The Floor / Off The Wall / Girlfriend / She's Out Of My Life / I Can't Help It / It's The Falling In Love / Burn This Disco Out*
LP, Cassette - Epic 1979 (CD Reissue - Epic 1987)

Thriller *Wanna Be Startin' Something / Baby Be Mine / The Girl Is Mine / Thriller / Beat It / Billie Jean / Human Nature / P.Y.T. (Pretty Young Thing) / The Lady In My Life*
LP, Cassette - Epic 1982 (CD Reissue - Epic 1987 / SACD Reissue - Sony 2001)

Bad *Bad / The Way You Make Me Feel / Speed Demon / Liberian Girl / Just Good Friends / Another Part Of Me / Man In The Mirror / I Just Can't Stop Loving You / Dirty Diana / Smooth Criminal / Leave Me Alone* (CD Only)
LP, Cassette, CD - Epic 1987

Dangerous *Jam / Why You Wanna Trip On Me / In The Closet / She Drives Me Wild / Remember The Time / Can't Let Her Get Away / Heal The World / Black Or White / Who Is It / Give In To Me / Will You Be There / Keep The Faith / Gone Too Soon / Dangerous*
LP, Cassette, CD - Epic 1991

HIStory *Billie Jean / The Way You Make Me Feel / Black Or White / Rock With You / She's Out Of My Life / Bad / I Just Can't Stop Loving You / Man In The Mirror / Thriller / Beat It / The Girl Is Mine / Remember The Time / Don't Stop 'Til You Get Enough / Wanna Be Startin' Something / Heal The World / Scream / They Don't Care About Us / Stranger In Moscow / This Time Around / Earth Song / D.S. / Money / Come Together / You Are Not Alone / Childhood / Tabloid Junkie / 2 Bad / HIStory / Little Susie / Smile*
LP, Cassette, CD - Epic 1995

Blood On The Dance Floor *Blood On The Dance Floor / Morphine / Superfly Sister / Ghosts / Is It Scary? / Scream Louder (Flyte Tyme Remix) / Money (Fire Island Radio Edit) / 2 Bad (Refugee Camp Mix) / Stranger In Moscow (Tee's In-House Club Mix) / This Time Around (DM Radio Mix) / Earth Song (Hani's Club Experience) / You Are Not Alone (Classic Club Mix) / HIStory (Tony Moran's HIStory Lesson)*
LP, CD, MD - Epic 1997

Invincible *Unbreakable / Heartbreaker / Invincible / Break Of Dawn / Heaven Can Wait / You Rock My World / Butterflies / Speechless / 2000 Watts / You Are My Life / Privacy / Don't Walk Away / Cry / The Lost Children / Whatever Happens / Threatened*
CD, MD - Sony/Epic - 2001

SOLO SINGLES

Got To Be There *Got To Be There /
Maria (You Were The Only One)*
7" - Tamla Motown 1972

Rockin' Robin *Rockin' Robin /
Love Is Here And Now You're Gone*
7" - Tamla Motown 1972

Ain't No Sunshine *Ain't No Sunshine /
I Wanna Be Where You Are*
7" - Tamla Motown 1972

Ben *Ben / You Can Cry On My Shoulder*
7" - Tamla Motown 1972

Morning Glow *Morning Glow / My Girl*
7" - Tamla Motown 1973

Music And Me *Music And Me / Johnny Raven*
7" - Tamla Motown 1974

One Day In Your Life *One Day In Your Life /
With A Child's Heart*
7" - Tamla Motown 1975

Just A Little Bit Of You *Just A Little Bit Of You
/ Dear Michael*
7" - Tamla Motown 1975

You Can't Win *You Can't Win (Parts 1 & 2)*
7", 12" - Tamla Motown 1979

Don't Stop 'Til You Get Enough *Don't Stop
'Til You Get Enough / I Can't Help It*
7" - Epic 1979

Don't Stop 'Til You Get Enough *Don't Stop
'Til You Get Enough / Don't Stop 'Til You Get
Enough (edit)*
7" - Epic 1979

Off The Wall *Off The Wall /
Working Day And Night*
7" - Epic 1979

Off The Wall *Off The Wall / Get On The Floor*
7" - Epic 1979

Off The Wall *Off The Wall / Rock With You*
7" - Epic 1979

Rock With You *Rock With You /
Get On The Floor*
7" - Epic 1980

Rock With You *Rock With You /
Working Day And Night*
7" - Epic 1980

Rock With You *Rock With You /
You Can't Win / Get On The Floor*
12" - Epic 1980

She's Out Of My Life *She's Out Of My Life /
Push Me Away* [With The Jacksons]
7" - Epic 1980

She's Out Of My Life *She's Out Of My Life /
Get On The Floor*
7" - Epic 1980

She's Out Of My Life *She's Out Of My Life /
Lovely One*
7" - Epic 1980

Ben *Ben / Abraham, Martin and John* (B-side by
Marvin Gaye)
7" - Motown 1980

Girlfriend *Girlfriend /
Bless His Soul* (With The Jacksons)
7" - Epic 1980

Got To Be There *Got To Be There /
I Miss You Baby*
7" - Tamla Motown 1980

One Day In Your Life *One Day In Your Life /
Take Me Back*
7" - Tamla Motown 1981

We're Almost There *We're Almost There /
We Got A Good Thing Going*
7", 12" - Tamla Motown 1981

Off The Wall *Off The Wall / Don't Stop Til You
Get Enough*
7" - Epic 1982

The Girl Is Mine *The Girl Is Mine /
Can't Get Outta The Rain*
7" - Epic 1982

Got To Be There *Got To Be There / Ben*
Cassette - Motown 1983

Billie Jean *Billie Jean / It's The Falling In Love*
7" - Epic 1983

Billie Jean *Billie Jean / Can't Get Outta The Rain*
7" - Epic 1983

Billie Jean *Billie Jean (Extended) / Billie Jean
(Instrumental) / It's The Falling In Love*
12" - Epic 1983

Beat It *Beat It / Burn This Disco Out*
7" - Epic 1983

Beat It *Beat It / Get On The Floor*
7" - Epic 1983

Beat It *Beat It / Get On The Floor /
Don't Stop 'Til You Get Enough (Edit)*
12" - Epic 1983

Wanna Be Startin' Something *Wanna Be
Startin' Something / Rock With You (Live)* [With
the Jacksons]
7" - Epic 1983

Wanna Be Startin' Something *Wanna Be
Startin' Something / Rock With You / Wanna Be
Startin' Somethin (Instrumental)*
12" - Epic 1983

Wanna Be Startin' Something *Wanna Be
Startin' Something / Wanna Be Startin' Something
(instrumental)*
7" - Epic 1983

Happy *Happy / We're Almost There*
7" (Picture Disc), 12" - Tamla Motown 1983

Human Nature *Human Nature / Baby Be Mine*
7" - Epic 1983

Pretty Young Thing (P.Y.T.) *P.Y.T. (Pretty
Young Thing)*
7" - Epic 1983

Pretty Young Thing (P.Y.T.) *P.Y.T. (Pretty
Young Thing) / Working Day And Night*
[With The Jacksons]
7" - Epic 1983

Pretty Young Thing (P.Y.T.) *P.Y.T. (Pretty
Young Thing) / Heartbreak Hotel*
7" - Epic 1984

Pretty Young Thing (P.Y.T.) *P.Y.T. (Pretty
Young Thing) / Heartbreak Hotel / Thriller*
7", 12" - Epic 1984

Thriller *Thriller / The Things I Do For You (Live)*
[With The Jacksons]
7" - Epic 1983 UK

Thriller *Thriller / Can't Get Outta The Rain*
7" - Epic 1983

Thriller *Thriller / Thriller (Special Edit) / The
Things I Do For You (Live)* [With The Jacksons]
12" - Epic 1983

Thriller *Thriller / Thriller (Instrumental)*
12" - Epic 1984

Farewell My Summer Love *Farewell My
Summer Love / Call On Me*
7", 12" - Tamla Motown 1984

Girl You're So Together *Girl You're So Together
/ Touch The One You Love*
7" - Tamla Motown 1984

Girl You're So Together *Girl You're So Together
/ Touch The One You Love / Ben / Ain't No
Sunshine*
12" - Tamla Motown 1984

Got To Be There *Got To Be There /
Rockin' Robin*
7", 12" - Motown 1985

I Just Can't Stop Loving You *I Just Can't Stop
Loving You / Baby Be Mine*
7", 12" - Epic 1987

I Just Can't Stop Loving You *I Just Can't Stop
Loving You*
CD - Epic 1987

Bad *Bad / I Can't Help It*
7" - Epic 1987

Bad *Bad / Bad (Dance Remix Radio Edit)*
7" - Epic 1987

Bad *Bad (Dance Extended Mix With False Fade) /
Bad (Dub Version) / Bad (A Capella)*
12" - Epic 1987

Bad *Bad (Dance Extended Mix With False Fade) /
Bad / Bad (Dance Remix Radio Edit) /
Bad (Dub Version) / Bad (A Capella)*
12" - Epic/Sony 1987

The Way You Make Me Feel *The Way You
Make Me Feel / The Way You Make Me Feel
(Instrumental)*
7" - Epic 1987

The Way You Make Me Feel *The Way You
Make Me Feel (Extended Dance Mix) /
The Way You Make Me Feel (Dub) /
The Way You Make Me Feel (A Capella)*
12" - Epic 1987

The Way You Make Me Feel *The Way You
Make Me Feel (Extended Dance Mix) /
The Way You Make Me Feel (Extended Dance Mix
Radio Edit) / The Way You Make Me Feel (Dub) /
The Way You Make Me Feel (A Capella)*
12" - Epic 1987

Man In The Mirror *Man In The Mirror (7"
Mix) / Man In The Mirror (Instrumental)*
7" - Epic 1988

Dirty Diana *Dirty Diana /
Dirty Diana (Instrumental)*
7", 12 " - Epic 1988

Another Part Of Me *Another Part Of Me /
Another Part Of Me (Instrumental)*
7" - Epic 1988

Another Part Of Me *Another Part Of Me
(Extended Dance Mix) / Another Part Of Me
(Radio Edit) / Another Part Of Me (Dub Mix) /
Another Part Of Me (A Capella)*
12" - Epic 1988

Got to Be There *Got to Be There /
Rockin' Robin / I Wanna Be Where You Are /
Just A Little Bit Of You*
CD - Motown 1989

Smooth Criminal *Smooth Criminal /
Smooth Criminal (Instrumental)*
7" - Epic 1989

Smooth Criminal *Smooth Criminal (Extended
Dance Mix) / Smooth Criminal (Dancemix - Dub
Version) / Smooth Criminal (A Capella)*
12" - Epic 1989

Smooth Criminal *Smooth Criminal (Extended
Dance Mix) / Smooth Criminal (Extended Dance
Mix Radio Edit) / Smooth Criminal (Dancemix -
Dub Version) / Smooth Criminal (A Capella)*
12" - Epic 1989

Leave Me Alone *Leave Me Alone*
7" - Epic 1989

Leave Me Alone *Leave Me Alone /
Don't Stop 'Til You Get Enough / Human Nature*
12" - Epic 1989

Liberian Girl *Liberian Girl (Edit) /
Get On The Floor / Girlfriend*
12" - Epic 1989

Black Or White *Black Or White (7") /
Black Or White (7" Instrumental)*
7", CD, Cassette - Epic 1991

Black Or White *Black Or White (The
Underground Club Mix) / Remember The Time*
7" - Epic 1991

Black Or White *Black Or White (7") /
Bad / Black Or White (7" Instrumental) / Thriller*
12" - Epic 1991

Black Or White *Black Or White (7") /
Black Or White (7" Instrumental) /
Smooth Criminal*
CD - Epic 1991

Black Or White *Black Or White (The Clivilles &
Cole House/Club Mix) / Black Or White (The
Clivilles & Cole House/Dub Mix) /
Black Or White (The Underground Club Mix) /
Black Or White (House With Guitar Radio Mix) /
Black Or White (Tribal Beats)*
12" - Epic 1991

Black Or White *Black Or White (The Clivilles &
Cole House/Club Mix) / Black Or White (The
Clivilles & Cole House/Dub Mix) /
Black Or White (The Underground Club Mix) /
Black Or White (House With Guitar Radio Mix) /
Black Or White (Tribal Beats)*
CD - Epic 1991

Black Or White *Black Or White (The Clivilles &
Cole House/Club Mix) / Black Or White (The
Clivilles & Cole House/Dub Mix) /
Black Or White (House With Guitar Radio Mix) /
Black Or White (7") / Black Or White (7"
Instrumental) / Black Or White (Tribal Beats)*
12" - Epic 1991

Someone Put Your Hand Out *Someone Put
Your Hand Out / Dangerous Medley (Bruce
Swedien)*
Cassette - Epic 1992

Remember The Time *Remember The Time (7")*
7" - Epic 1992

Remember The Time *Remember The Time (7")
/ Remember The Time (Silky Soul 7") /
Remember The Time (New Jack Main Mix) /
Remember The Time (12" Main Mix) /
Remember The Time (New Jack Mix) /
Remember The Time (Silky Soul 12" Mix) /
Remember The Time (Silky Soul Dub) /
Remember The Time (E-Smoove's Late Nite Mix) /
Come Together*
CD - Epic 1992

Remember The Time *Remember The Time (7")
/ Remember The Time (Silky Soul 7") / Remember
The Time (New Jack Main Mix) / Come Together*
CD - Epic 1992

Remember The Time *Remember The Time
(Silky Soul 7") / Remember The Time (New Jack
Radio Mix) / Remember The Time (12" Main Mix)
/ Remember The Time (E-Smoove's Late Nite Mix)
/ Remember The Time (Maurice's Underground) /
Black Or White (Clivilles & Cole Radio Mix) /
Black Or White (House With Guitar Radio Mix) /
Black Or White (Clivilles & Cole Club Mix) /
Black Or White (The Underground Club Mix)*
CD - Epic 1992

Remember The Time *Remember The Time
(Silky Soul 12" Mix) / Remember The Time (E-
Smoove's Late Nite Mix) / Remember The Time
(Silky Soul Dub) / Remember The Time (12" Main
Mix) / Black Or White (The Underground Club
Mix)*
12" - Epic 1992

In The Closet *In The Closet (7" Edit) / In The
Closet (Radio Edit)*
7" - Epic 1992

In The Closet *In The Closet (7" Edit) /
In The Closet (Club Mix) / In The Closet (The
Underground Mix) / In The Closet (Touch Me
Dub) / In The Closet (Ki's 12") / In The Closet
(The Promise)*
CD - Epic 1992

In The Closet *In The Closet (Club Edit) / In The
Closet (The Underground Mix) / In The Closet
(The Promise) / In The Closet (The Wow) /
Remember The Time (New Jack Jazz)*
CD - Epic 1992

In The Closet *In The Closet (7" Edit) / In The
Closet (Radio Edit) / In The Closet (Ki's 12") / In
The Closet (Freestyle Mix) / In The Closet (The
Newark Mix)*
CD - Epic 1992

In The Closet *In The Closet (Club Edit) /
In The Closet (The Newark Mix) / In The Closet
(The Promise) / In The Closet (The Wow) /
Remember The Time (New Jack Jazz)*
CD - Epic 1992

In The Closet *In The Closet (Club Mix) /
In The Closet (The Underground Mix) / In The
Closet (Touch Me Dub) / In The Closet (Ki's 12")*
CD - Epic 1992

In The Closet *In The Closet (The Mission) /
In The Closet (Freestyle Mix) / In The Closet (Mix
Of Life) / In The Closet (Underground Dub)*
12" - Epic 1992

In The Closet *In The Closet (The Mission) / In The Closet (Freestyle Mix) / In The Closet (Mix Of Life) / In The Closet (Underground Dub)*
CD - Epic 1992

Who Is It *Who Is It*
7" - Epic 1992

Who Is It *Who Is It (7" Edit With Intro) / Who Is It (The Most Patient Mix) / Who Is It (IHS Mix) / Who Is It (P-Man Dub) / Don't Stop 'Til You Get Enough (Roger's U-ground Solution Mix)*
CD - Epic 1992

Who Is It *Who Is It (Patience Mix) / Who Is It (The Most Patient Mix) / Who Is It (IHS Mix) / Who Is It (P-Man Dub)*
12" - Epic 1992

Who Is It *Who Is It (Patience Mix) / Who Is It (The Most Patient Mix) / Who Is It (IHS Mix) / Who Is It (P-Man Dub) / Don't Stop 'Til You Get Enough (Roger's U-ground Solution Mix)*
CD - Epic 1992

Who Is It *Who Is It (Oprah Winfrey Special In.) / Who Is It (Patience Edit) / Who Is It (Brother's In Rhythm House 7") / Who Is It (Brother's In Rhythm House Mix) / Beat It (Moby's Sub Mix)*
CD - Epic 1993

Who Is It *Who Is It (Brother's In Rhythm House Mix) / Who Is It (Tribal Version) / Who Is It (Moby's Sub Mix) / Who Is It (Lakeside Dub) / Beat It (Moby's Sub Mix)*
12" - Epic 1993

Who Is It *Who Is It (7" Edit With Intro) / Who Is It (The Most Patient Mix) / Who Is It (IHS Mix) / Who Is It (P-Man Dub) / Who Is It (Brother's In Rhythm House Mix) / Who Is It (Tribal Version) / Who Is It (Moby's Sub Mix) / Who Is It (Lakeside Dub) Who Is It (Patience Mix) Who Is It (Patience Edit) Who Is It (Brother's In Rhythm House 7")*
Double 12" - Epic 1992

Jam *Jam (7" Edit) / Beat It (Moby's Sub Mix)*
7" - Epic 1992

Jam *Jam (7" Edit) / Rock With You (Masters At Work Remix)*
7" - Epic 1992

Jam *Jam (7" Edit) / Jam (Roger's Jeep Mix) / Jam (Atlanta Techno Dub) / Wanna Be Startin' Something (Brothers In Rhythm House Mix)*
CD - Epic 1992

Jam *Jam (Roger's Jeep Radio Mix) / Jam (Silky 7") / Jam (Roger's Club Mix) / Jam (Atlanta Techno Mix) / Rock With You (Masters At Work Remix)*
CD - Epic 1992

Jam *Jam (Roger's Jeep Radio Mix) / Jam (Teddy's Jam) / Jam (More Than Enuff Mix) / Jam (Atlanta Techno Mix) / Don't Stop 'Til You Get Enough (Roger's U-ground Solution Mix)*
CD - Epic 1992

Jam *Jam (Roger's Club Mix) / Jam (Silky 7") / Jam (E-Smoove's Jazzy Jam) /Jam (Video Mix) / Beat It (Moby's Sub Mix)*
CD - Epic 1992

Jam *Jam (Roger's Club Mix) / Jam (More Than Enuff Mix) / Jam (E-Smoove's Jazzy Jam) / Jam (Teddy's Jam) / Jam (Roger's Underground Mix) / Jam (Silky 12")*
12" - Epic 1992

Jam *Jam (Roger's Club Mix) / Jam (Atlanta Techno Mix) / Jam (Teddy's Jam) / Jam (Roger's Jeep Mix) / Jam (E-Smoove's Jazzy Jam) / Don't Stop 'Til You Get Enough (Roger's U-ground Solution Mix)*
12" - Epic 1992

Heal The World *Heal The World (7" Edit) / She Drives Me Wild*
7" - Epic 1992

Heal The World *Heal The World (7" Edit) / Heal The World (7" Edit With Intro) / Heal The World (LP Version) / She Drives Me Wild*
CD - Epic 1992

Heal The World *Heal The World (7" Edit) / Heal The World (7" Edit With Intro)*
CD - Epic 1992

Give In To Me *Give In To Me / Dirty Diana (Edit)*
7" - Epic 1993

Give In To Me *Dirty Diana (Edit) / Beat It*
CD - Epic 1993

Bonus CD Sampler (Promo) *Who Is It (IHS Mix) / Black Or White (The Clivilles & Cole House/Club Mix) / Jam (Teddy's Jam) / In The Closet (The Mission) / Give In To Me (Vocal Version) / Remember The Time (Silky Soul 12" Mix) / Rock With You (Masters At Work Remix) / Don't Stop 'Til You Get Enough (Roger's U-ground Solution Mix)*
CD - Epic 1993

Will You Be There *Will You Be There (Edit) / Will You Be There (Instrumental)*
Cassette - Epic 1993

Will You Be There *Will You Be There (Edit) / Man In The Mirror / Girlfriend / Will You Be There*
CD - Epic 1993

Gone Too Soon *Gone Too Soon / Gone Too Soon (Instrumental)*
7" - Epic 1993

Gone Too Soon *Gone Too Soon / Human Nature / She's Out Of My Life / Thriller*
CD - Epic 1993

Scream *Scream (Single Edit) / Childhood*
7", Cassette, CD - Epic 1995

Scream [Promo] *Scream (Single Edit)*
CD - Epic 1995

Scream [Promo] *Scream (Single Edit With Spoken Intro) / Hits Medley*
CD - Epic 1995

Scream [Limited Edition Poster Bag] *Scream (Def Radio Mix) / Scream (Single Edit)*
7" - Epic 1995

Scream
Scream (Single Edit) / Scream (Def Radio Mix) / Scream (Naughty Radio Edit With Rap) / Scream (Dave "Jam" Hall's Urban Remix Edit) / Childhood
CD - Epic 1995

Scream *Scream (Naughty Radio Edit With Rap) / Scream (Dave "Jam" Hall's Urban Remix Edit) / Scream (D.M. R&B Radio Mix) / Scream (Single Edit Number Two) / Scream (Naughty Main Mix) / Scream (Dave "Jam" Hall's Extended Urban Remix) / Scream (D.M. R&B Extended Mix) / Childhood*
Cassette -Epic 1995

Scream *Scream (Single Edit Number Two) / Scream (Def Radio Mix) / Scream (Naughty Radio Edit With Rap) / Scream (Dave "Jam" Hall's Extended Urban Remix) / Scream (Classic Club Mix) / Childhood*
CD - Epic 1995

Scream *Scream (Single Edit) / Scream (Naughty Pretty-Pella) / Scream (Naughty Main Mix Without Rap) / Scream (Pressurized Dub Pt. Two)*
CD - Epic 1995

Scream *Scream (Naughty Main Mix) / Scream (Naughty Pretty-Pella) / Scream (Pressurized Dub Pt. Two) / Scream (Album Version)*
12" - Epic 1995

Scream *Scream (Classic Club Mix) / Scream (Pressurized Dub Pt. One) / Scream (D.M. R&B Extended Mix) / Scream (Dave "Jam" Hall's Extended Remix Edit) / Scream (Naughty Main Mix) / Scream (Single Edit Number Two)*
CD - Epic 1995

Scream [Promo; "Scream The Remix Edits"] *Scream (Naughty Radio Edit With Rap) / Scream (Naughty Radio Edit Without Rap) / Scream (Dave "Jam" Hall's Urban Remix Edit) / Scream (Def Radio Mix) / Scream (Single Edit) / Childhood*
CD - Epic 1995

Scream *Scream (Clean Album Version) / Scream (Single Edit Number Two) / Scream (D.M. R&B Extended Mix) / Scream (Naughty Radio Edit With Rap) / Childhood*
CD - Epic 1995

Scream *Scream (Classic Club Mix) / Scream (Pressurized Dub Pt. One) / Scream (D.M. R&B Extended Mix) / Scream (Dave "Jam" Hall's Extended Urban Remix) / Scream (Naughty Main Mix) / Scream (Naughty A Capella)*
12" - Epic 1995

Scream *Scream (Classic Club Mix) / Scream (D.M. R&B Extended Mix) / Scream (Def Radio Mix) / Scream (Naughty Main Mix) / Scream (Naughty Main Mix Without Rap) / Scream (Dave "Jam" Hall's Extended Urban Remix)*
12" - Epic 1995

Scream *Scream (Classic Club Mix) / Scream (Pressurized Dub Pt. One) / Scream (Naughty Main Mix) / Scream (Dave "Jam" Hall's Extended Urban Remix) / Scream (Single Edit Number Two) / Childhood*
12" - Epic 1995

Scream *Scream (Pressurized Dub Part One) / Scream (Pressurized Dub Part Two) / Scream (Album Version) / Scream (Single Edit Number Two) / Scream (Naughty Pretty-Pella) / Scream (Naughty A Capella)*
12" - Epic 1995

Scream Megamix *Megamix / Megamix / Scream (Dave "Jam" Hall's Urban Remix) / Scream (Instrumental)*
12" - Epic 1995

You Are Not Alone *You Are Not Alone (Radio Edit) / You Are Not Alone (Scream Louder Flyte Tyme Remix)*
7", CD - Epic 1995

You Are Not Alone [Promo] - *You Are Not Alone (Radio Edit) / You Are Not Alone*
CD - Epic 1995

You Are Not Alone [Promo] - *You Are Not Alone (Album Edit) / You Are Not Alone (Radio Edit) / You Are Not Alone*
CD - Epic 1995

You Are Not Alone *You Are Not Alone (Radio Edit) / You Are Not Alone (Franctified Club Mix) / You Are Not Alone (Classic Song Version) / You Are Not Alone (Jon B. Main Mix) / You Are Not Alone (Jon B. Padapella mix)*
CD - Epic 1995

You Are Not Alone *You Are Not Alone (Radio Edit) / You Are Not Alone (Franctified Club Mix) / You Are Not Alone (Classic Song Version) / You Are Not Alone (Jon B. Main Mix) / You Are Not Alone (Jon B. Padapella Mix) / Magic Michael Jackson Mix*
CD - Epic 1995

You Are Not Alone *You Are Not Alone / You Are Not Alone (R. Kelly Remix) / Rock With You (Masters At Work Remix) / Rock With You (Frankie's Favorite Club Mix)*
CD - Epic 1995

You Are Not Alone [Promo] *Rock With You (Masters At Work Remix) / Rock With You (Frankie's Favorite Club Mix)*
12" - Epic 1995

You Are Not Alone [Promo] *Rock With You (Frankie's Favorite Club Mix Radio Edit) / Rock With You (Frankie's Favorite Club Mix)*
CD - Epic 1995

You Are Not Alone *You Are Not Alone (Radio Edit) / You Are Not Alone (R. Kelly Remix) / Rock With You (Masters At Work Remix) / Rock With You (Frankie's Favorite Club Mix)*
CD - Epic 1995

You Are Not Alone [Promo] *You Are Not Alone (R. Kelly Remix Edit) / You Are Not Alone (Classic Club Edit) / You Are Not Alone (Jon B. Remix Edit) / You Are Not Alone (R. Kelly Remix)*
CD - Epic 1995

You Are Not Alone *You Are Not Alone (Radio Edit) / You Are Not Alone (Franctified Club Mix) - You Are Not Alone (Classic Song Version) / You Are Not Alone (Jon B. Main Mix) / MJ Medley / You Are Not Alone (Jon B. Padapella Mix)*
CD - Epic 1995

You Are Not Alone *You Are Not Alone (R. Kelly Remix) / You Are Not Alone (Jon B. Main Mix) / Rock With You (Masters At Work Remix) / You Are Not Alone (Franctified Club Mix) / Rock With You (Frankie's Favorite Club Mix)*
12" - Epic 1995

You Are Not Alone [Promo] *You Are Not Alone (R. Kelly Remix) / You Are Not Alone (Jon B. Main Mix) / You Are Not Alone (Jon B. Padapella Mix) / You Are Not Alone (Franctified Club Mix)*
CD - Epic 1995

You Are Not Alone *You Are Not Alone (Radio Edit) / You Are Not Alone (Classic Song Version) / You Are Not Alone (Jon B. Main Mix) / You Are Not Alone (R. Kelly Remix) / Scream Louder (Flyte Tyme Remix) / Rock With You (Frankie's Favorite Club Mix)*
CD - Epic 1995

You Are Not Alone *You Are Not Alone (Album Edit) / You Are Not Alone (Radio Edit) / You Are Not Alone (Franctified Club Mix) / Scream Louder (Flyte Tyme Remix) / MJ Megaremix*
CD - Epic 1995

You Are Not Alone *You Are Not Alone (Franctified Club Mix) / You Are Not Alone / MJ Megaremix / Scream Louder (Flyte Tyme Remix)*
12" - Epic 1995

You Are Not Alone *You Are Not Alone (Album Edit) / You Are Not Alone (Radio Edit) / You Are Not Alone (Franctified Club Mix) / You Are Not Alone (R. Kelly Remix) / You Are Not Alone (Classic Song Version) / You Are Not Alone (Jon B. Main Mix) / You Are Not Alone (Jon B. Padapella Mix)*
CD - Epic 1995

You Are Not Alone *You Are Not Alone (Classic Club Edit) / You Are Not Alone (Classic Club Mix) / You Are Not Alone (Franctified Club Mix) / Scream (Def Radio Mix) / Scream (Def Extended Remix)*
CD - Epic 1995

You Are Not Alone [Promo] *You Are Not Alone (Franctified Club Mix) / You Are Not Alone (Knuckluv Dub)*
12" - Epic 1995

You Are Not Alone [Promo] *You Are Not Alone (Franctified Club Mix) / You Are Not Alone / You Are Not Alone (Knuckluv Dub) / You Are Not Alone (Classic Club Mix)*
12" - Epic 1995

Earth Song *Earth Song (Radio Edit) / MJ Megaremix*
CD - Epic 1995

Earth Song *Earth Song (Radio Edit) / Earth Song (Hani's Extended Radio Experience)*
Cassette - Epic 1995

Earth Song *Earth Song (Radio Edit) / This Time Around / Earth Song*
CD - Epic 1995

Earth Song *Earth Song / Earth Song (Hani's Radio Experience) / Earth Song (Hani's Around The World Experience) / You Are Not Alone (Knuckluv Dub) / MJ Megaremix*
CD - Epic 1995

Earth Song [Promo] *Earth Song (Hani's Around The World Experience) / Earth Song (Hani's Club Experience) / Earth Song (Hani's Extended Radio Experience) / Earth Song (Hani's Radio Experience)*
12" - Epic 1995

Earth Song *Earth Song (Radio Edit) / Earth Song (Hani's Extended Radio Experience) / Wanna Be Startin' Something (Tommy D's Main Mix) / Wanna Be Startin' Something (Brothers In Rhythm House Mix)*
CD - Epic 1995

Earth Song *Earth Song (Hani's Around The World Experience) / Wanna Be Startin' Something (Tommy D's Main Mix) / Wanna Be Startin' Something (Brothers In Rhythm House Mix)*
12" - Epic 1995

Earth Song [CD 1] *Earth Song (Radio Edit) / Earth Song (Hani's Club Experience) / DMC Megamix*
CD - Epic 1995

Earth Song [CD 2] *Earth Song (Radio Edit) / Earth Song (Hani's Radio Experience) / Wanna Be Startin' Something (Brother's In Rhythm House Mix) / Wanna Be Startin' Something (Tommy D's Main Mix)*
CD - Epic 1995

Earth Song [Promo] *Earth Song (Radio Edit) / Earth Song / Earth Song (Hani's Radio Experience)*
CD - Epic 1995

Earth Song [Promo] *Earth Song (Hani's Club Experience) / Earth Song / Earth Song (Hani's Radio Experience) / Earth Song (Hani's Around The World Experience)*
12" - Epic 1995

This Time Around [Promo] *This Time Around (Dallas Clean Album Remix) / This Time Around (David Mitson Clean Album) / This Time Around (Dallas Radio Remix) / This Time Around (Dallas Radio Remix Without Rap) / This Time Around (Maurice's Hip Hop Around Mix (w/Drop)) / This Time Around (Maurice's Hip Hop Around Mix Without Rap) / This Time Around (Maurice's Club Around Radio Mix) / This Time Around (D.M. Radio Mix) / Earth Song (Radio Edit) / Earth Song (Hani's Radio Experience)*
CD - Epic 1995

This Time Around [Promo] *This Time Around (D.M. Mad Club Mix) / This Time Around (D.M. Radio Mix) / This Time Around (Maurice's Club Around Mix) / This Time Around (Georgie's House 'N' Around Mix) / This Time Around (The Timeland Dub) / This Time Around (The Neverland Dub (Aftermath)) / This Time Around (The Don's Control This Dub) / This Time Around (UBQ's Opera Vibe dub) / This Time Around (D.M. Bang Da Drums Mix)*
Double 12" - Epic 1995

This Time Around [Promo] *This Time Around (Dallas Main Extended Mix) / This Time Around (Maurice's Hip Hop Around Mix) / This Time Around (Maurice's Hip Hop Around Mix Without Rap) / This Time Around (Dallas Main Mix) / This Time Around (Dallas Main Mix Without Rap) / This Time Around (Album Instrumental)*
12" - Epic 1995

This Time Around [Promo] *This Time Around (Uno Clio 12" Master Mix) / This Time Around (D.M. AM Mix) / This Time Around (D.M. Mad Dub) / This Time Around (Uno Clio Dub Mix)*
12" - Epic 1995

They Don't Care About Us *They Don't Care About Us (Single Version) / They Don't Care About Us (L. To I.'s Walk In The Park Edit)*
Cassette, CD - Epic 1996

They Don't Care About Us *They Don't Care About Us (LP Edit) / They Don't Care About Us (L. To I.'s Walk In The Park Mix) / They Don't Care About Us (L. To I. Classic Paradise Mix) / They Don't Care About Us (L. To I.'s Anthem Of Love Mix) / They Don't Care About Us (Love To Infinity's Hacienda Mix) / They Don't Care About Us (Dallas Main Mix)*
TC - Epic 1996

They Don't Care About Us *They Don't Care About Us (L. To I.'s Walk In The Park Mix) / They Don't Care About Us (L. To I. Classic Paradise Mix) / They Don't Care About Us (L. To I.'s Anthem Of Love Mix) / They Don't Care About Us (Love To Infinity's Hacienda Mix) / They Don't Care About Us (Dallas Main Mix)*
12" - Epic 1996

They Don't Care About Us *They Don't Care About Us (LP Edit) / They Don't Care About Us (L. To I.'s Walk In The Park Mix) / They Don't Care About Us (L. To I.'s Anthem Of Love Mix) / They Don't Care About Us (Love To Infinity's Hacienda Mix) / They Don't Care About Us (Dallas Main Mix)*
CD - Epic 1996

They Don't Care About Us [Promo] *They Don't Care About Us (Track Master's Remix) / They Don't Care About Us (Dallas Main Mix) / They Don't Care About Us (Charles Full Dirty Mix) / They Don't Care About Us (LP Edit) / They Don't Care About Us (L. To I.'s Walk In The Park Mix) / They Don't Care About Us (Track Master's Instrumental)*
12" - Epic 1996

They Don't Care About Us *They Don't Care About Us (Single Version) / They Don't Care About Us (Track Master's Remix) / They Don't Care About Us (Charles Full Joint Remix) / Beat It (Moby's Sub Mix)*
CD - Epic 1996

They Don't Care About Us *They Don't Care About Us (Single Version) / They Don't Care About Us (Track Master's Remix) / Beat It (Moby's Sub Mix)*
CD - Epic 1996

They Don't Care About Us *They Don't Care About Us (Single Version) / They Don't Care About Us (Track Master's Remix) / They Don't Care About Us (Charles Full Joint Remix) / Beat It (Moby's Sub Mix)* - This release also includes the video to Earth Song on CD-ROM.
CD - Epic 1996

They Don't Care About Us *They Don't Care About Us (Single Version) / Rock With You (Frankie's Favorite Club Mix Radio Edit) / Earth Song (Hani's Radio Experience) / Wanna Be Startin' Something (Brother's In Rhythm House Mix)*
CD - Epic 1996

They Don't Care About Us *They Don't Care About Us (Single Version) / They Don't Care About Us (Charles' Full Joint Mix (No Intro)) / Rock With You (Frankie's Favorite Club Mix Radio Edit) / Earth Song (Hani's Radio Experience)*
Cassette - Epic 1996

They Don't Care About Us [Promo] *They Don't Care About Us (Single Version) / They Don't Care About Us (Charles' Full Joint Mix (No Intro)) / They Don't Care About Us (L. To I.'s Walk In The Park Edit) / They Don't Care About Us (Track Master's Radio Remix)*
CD - Epic 1996

They Don't Care About Us *They Don't Care About Us (Single Version) / They Don't Care About Us (Charles Full Joint Remix) / They Don't Care About Us (Dallas Main Mix) / They Don't Care About Us (L. To I.'s Walk In The Park Edit) / They Don't Care About Us (L. To I. Classic Paradise Radio Mix) / They Don't Care About Us (Track Master's Radio Remix) / Rock With You (Frankie's Favorite Club Mix) / Earth Song (Hani's Club Experience)*
CD - Epic 1996

They Don't Care About Us [Promo] *They Don't Care About Us (L. To I. Classic Paradise Mix) / They Don't Care About Us (L. To I.'s Anthem Of Love Mix) / They Don't Care About Us (Dallas Main Mix) / They Don't Care About Us (Charles' Full Joint Mix (No Intro)) / They Don't Care About Us (Track Master's Remix) / They Don't Care About Us (Love To Infinity's Hacienda Mix) / They Don't Care About Us (L. To I.'s Walk In The Park Mix) / They Don't Care About Us (Single Version) / They Don't Care About Us (Charles' Full Joint mix (No Rap)) / They Don't Care About Us (A Capella)*
Double 12" - Epic 1996

Stranger In Moscow [Promo] *Stranger In Moscow (Radio Edit)*
CD - Epic 1996

Stranger In Moscow *Stranger In Moscow (Album Version) / Stranger In Moscow (Basement Boys 12" Dance Club Mix) / Stranger In Moscow (Hani's Num Club Mix) / Stranger In Moscow (Basement Boys Danger Dub) / Stranger In Moscow (Hani's Num Radio) / Stranger In Moscow (Basement Boys Radio Mix)*
CD - Epic 1996

Stranger In Moscow *Stranger In Moscow (Album Version) / Stranger In Moscow (Charles Roane - Full Mix W/Mute Drop) / Stranger In Moscow (Tee's Light AC Mix) / Stranger In Moscow (Tee's Freeze Radio) / Stranger In Moscow (Tee's In-House Club Mix) / Stranger In Moscow (TNT Frozen Sun Mix-Club) - CD 1*
CD - Epic 1996

Stranger In Moscow *Stranger In Moscow (Tee's Radio Mix) / Stranger In Moscow (Tee's In-House Club Mix) / Stranger In Moscow (TNT Frozen Sun Mix-Club) / Stranger In Moscow (Tee's Freeze Radio) / Stranger In Moscow (TNT Danger Dub) / Stranger In Moscow (Tee's Light AC Mix) - CD 2*
CD - Epic 1996

Stranger In Moscow *Stranger In Moscow (Album Version) / Stranger In Moscow (Charles Roane Full Mix) / Stranger In Moscow (Hani's Extended Chill Hop Mix) / Stranger In Moscow (Basement Boys Spensane Vocal Remix) / Stranger In Moscow (Hani's Dub Hop Mix) - CD 3*
CD - Epic 1996

Stranger In Moscow *Stranger In Moscow (Album Version) / Stranger In Moscow (Todd Terry Tee's Radio Mix) / Stranger In Moscow (Basement Boys 12" Dance Club Mix)*
CD - Epic 1996

Stranger In Moscow [Promo] *Stranger In Moscow (Todd Terry - Tee's Radio Mix) / Stranger In Moscow (Todd Terry - Tee's Freeze Radio) / Stranger In Moscow (Basement Boys - Radio Mix) / Stranger In Moscow (Charles Roane - Full Mix w/mute Drop) / Stranger In Moscow (Album Version)*
CD - Epic 1996

Stranger In Moscow [Promo] *Stranger In Moscow (Hani's Num Club) / Stranger In Moscow (Hani's Num Dub) / Stranger In Moscow (Hani's Extended Chill Hop) / Stranger In Moscow (Hani's Dub Hop) / Stranger In Moscow (Basement Boys 12" Dance Club Mix) / Stranger In Moscow (Basement Boys Spensane Vocal Remix) / Stranger In Moscow (Basement Boys Lonely Dub) / Stranger In Moscow (Basement Boys Danger Dub) / Stranger In Moscow (Basement Boys Bonus Dub Beets)*
Double 12" - Epic 1996

Stranger In Moscow [Promo] *Stranger In Moscow (Freeze Mix - Club) / Stranger In Moscow (Tee's Mission Mix-Club) / Stranger In Moscow (Tee's Bonus Beets Dub) / Stranger In Moscow (In House Club Mix) / Stranger In Moscow (Tee's Capella A'Capella) / Stranger In Moscow (TNT Frozen Sun Mix-Club) / Stranger In Moscow (TNT Danger Dub)*
Double 12" - Epic 1996

Stranger In Moscow *Stranger In Moscow (Basement Boys 12" Dance Club Mix) / Stranger In Moscow (Basement Boys Danger Dub) / Stranger In Moscow (Charles Roane Full Mix) / Stranger In Moscow (Hani's Num Club) / Stranger In Moscow (Hani's Extended Chill Hop) / Stranger In Moscow (Basement Boys Spensane Vocal Remix)*
12" - Epic 1996

Stranger In Moscow *Stranger In Moscow (Todd Terry's Freeze Mix-Club) / Stranger In Moscow (Todd Terry's Mission Mix-Club) / Stranger In Moscow (Todd Terry's Light AC Mix) / Stranger In Moscow (Todd Terry's In House Club Mix) / Stranger In Moscow (Todd Terry's Frozen Sun Mix-Club) / Stranger In Moscow (Tees Capella A'Capella)*
12" - Epic 1996

Blood On The Dance Floor *Blood On The Dance Floor / Blood On The Dance Floor (Refugee Camp Edit) / Dangerous (Roger's Dangerous Edit)*
TC - Epic 1997

Blood On The Dance Floor *Blood On The Dance Floor / Blood On The Dance Floor (TM's Switchblade Edit Short) / Dangerous (Roger's Dangerous Edit)*
CD - Epic 1997

Blood On The Dance Floor *Blood On The Dance Floor / Blood On The Dance Floor (Fire Island Vocal Mix) / Blood On The Dance Floor (TM's Switchblade Mix Short) / Dangerous (Roger's Dangerous Club Mix)*
CD - Epic 1997

Blood On The Dance Floor *Blood On The Dance Floor / Blood On The Dance Floor (TM's Switchblade Mix Short) / Blood On The Dance Floor (Refugee Camp Mix) / Blood On The Dance Floor (Fire Island Vocal Mix) / Blood On The Dance Floor (Fire Island Dub)*
CD - Epic 1997

Blood On The Dance Floor *Blood On The Dance Floor / Blood On The Dance Floor (TM's Switchblade Edit Short) / Blood On The Dance Floor (Refugee Camp Edit) / Blood On The Dance Floor (Fire Island Radio Edit)*
CD - Epic 1997

Blood On The Dance Floor *Blood On The Dance Floor / Blood On The Dance Floor (Refugee Camp Mix) / Blood On The Dance Floor (Refugee Camp Edit) / Dangerous (Roger's Dangerous Edit) / Blood On The Dance Floor (Fire Island Vocal Mix) / Blood On The Dance Floor (Fire Island Radio Edit) / Blood On The Dance Floor (TM's Switchblade Mix Short) / Blood On The Dance Floor (TM's Switchblade Edit Short)*
Double 12" - Epic 1997

Blood On The Dance Floor *Blood On The Dance Floor (Fire Island Vocal Mix) / Blood On The Dance Floor (Fire Island Radio Edit) / Blood On The Dance Floor (TM's Switchblade Mix Short) / Blood On The Dance Floor (TM's Switchblade Edit Short)*
12" - Epic 1996

Blood On The Dance Floor *Blood On The Dance Floor (TM's O-Postive Dub) / Blood On The Dance Floor (Fire Island Dub) / Dangerous (Roger's Dangerous Club Mix) / Dangerous (Roger's Rough Dub)*
12" - Epic 1996

Blood On The Dance Floor *Blood On The Dance Floor / Blood On The Dance Floor (TM's Switchblade Edit - Long) / Blood On The Dance Floor (Refugee Camp Edit) / Blood On The Dance Floor (Fire Island Radio Edit) / Blood On The Dance Floor (TM's Switchblade Mix Long) / Dangerous (Roger's Dangerous Club Mix)*
CD - Epic 1997

Blood On The Dance Floor *Blood On The Dance Floor (TM's Switchblade Mix Long) / Blood On The Dance Floor (Refugee Camp Edit) / Blood On The Dance Floor (Fire Island Vocal Mix) / Dangerous (Roger's Rough Dub)*
12" - Epic 1996

HIStory/Ghosts *HIStory (Tony Moran's 7" HIStory Lesson Edit) / HIStory (Radio Edit) / Ghosts (Radio Edit)*
Cassette - Epic 1997

HIStory/Ghosts *HIStory (Tony Moran's 7" HIStory Lesson Edit) / HIStory (Radio Edit) / Ghosts (Radio Edit) / Ghosts (Mousse T's Club Mix)*
CD - Epic 1997 [CD 1]

HIStory/Ghosts *HIStory (Tony Moran's HIStory Lesson) / HIStory (Tony Moran's HIStorical Dub) / HIStory (MARK!'s Vocal Club Mix) / HIStory (The Ummah Radio Mix) / HIStory (The Ummah Urban Mix)*
CD - Epic 1997 [CD 2]

HIStory/Ghosts *HIStory (7" HIStory Lesson Mix) / HIStory (MARKS! Radio Edit) / HIStory (MARKS! Vocal Club Mix) / HIStory (Unmah Radio Mix) / HIStory (Unmah DJ Mix) / HIStory (Unmak Main A Capella) / Ghosts (Radio Edit)*
CD - Epic 1997

HIStory/Ghosts *HIStory (MARKS! Vocal Club Mix) / HIStory (MARKS! Keep Movin' Dub) / HIStory (Unmah DJ Mix) / HIStory (Unmak Main A Capella) / Ghosts*
12" - Epic 1996

HIStory/Ghosts *HIStory (7" HIStory Lesson Mix) / Ghosts (Mousse T's Radio Edit) / Ghosts (Mousse T's Club Mix) / Ghosts (Radio Edit) / HIStory (TM's Historical Dub)*
CD - Epic 1997 [Full size jewelbox, 3 postcards + sticker]

HIStory/Ghosts *Ghosts (Mousse T's Club Mix) / Ghosts (Mousse T's Radio Rock) / HIStory (7" HIStory Lesson Mix) / HIStory (TM's Historical Dub)*
12" - Epic 1997

You Rock My World *Intro / You Rock My World (Album Version) / You Rock My World (Radio Edit)*
CD - Epic 2001

MICHAELJACKSONYOUROCKMYWORLD

You Rock My World *You Rock My World (12 "Remix) / You Rock My World (Album Version) / You Rock My World (Radio Version)*
12" - Epic 2001

Cry *Cry / Shout / Streetwalker / Cry (Short Film)*
CD - MJJ Music 2001

Cry *Cry / Cry (Album Version) / Streetwalker / Shout*
12" - Epic 2001

Remember The Time *Remember The Time (Silky Soul 7") / Remember The Time (New Jack Radio Mix) / Remember The Time (12" Main Mix) / Remember The Time (E-Smoove's Late Nite Mix)/ Remember The Time (Maurice's Underground) / Black Or White (The Clivilles & Cole Radio Mix) / Black Or White (House With Guitar Radio Mix) / Black Or White (The Clivilles & Cole House/Club Mix) / Black Or White (The Underground Club Mix)*
CD - Epic 2001

Butterflies *Butterflies (Album Version) / Butterflies (Master Mix Featuring Eve) /Butterflies (Instrumental)*
CD - Epic 2002

Butterflies *Butterflies (Master Mix Featuring Eve) / Butterflies (Album Version) / Butterflies (Instrumental) / Butterflies (Michael A Cappella)*
12" - Epic 2002

MICHAEL JACKSON GUEST APPEARANCES

The Wiz *A Brand New Day / Ease On Down The Road / Be a Lion*
LP - Motown 1978

Hotter Than July *All I Do* - Stevie Wonder + Michael Jackson (Vocals)
LP, CD - Motown 1980

Love Lives Forever - *I'm in Love Again* Minnie Ripperton + Michael Jackson (Vocals)
LP - Capitol 1980

Sometimes Late at Night *Just Friends* - Carole Bayer Sager + Michael Jackson (Backing Vocals)
LP - Epic 1980

LaToya Jackson *Night Time Lover* - Michael credited as producer and arranger
LP - Polydor 1980

Old Crest On The Wave *Save Me* - Dave Mason + Michael Jackson (Backing Vocals)
LP - CBS 1980

Keep The Fire *Who's Right Who's Wrong* - Kenny Loggins + Michael Jackson (Backing Vocals)
LP - CBS 1980

Light Up The Night *This Had To Be* - Brothers Johnson + Michael Jackson (Co-Writer and Backing Vocals)
LP - A&M 1980

The Dude *The Dude* - Quincy Jones + Michael Jackson (Backing Vocals)
LP - A&M 1981

Share Your Love *Goin' Back to Alabama* - Kenny Rogers + Michael Jackson (Backing Vocals)
LP - Liberty 1981

Sometimes Late At Night *Just Friends* - Carole Bayer Sager + Michael Jackson (Backing Vocals)
LP - Broadwalk 1981

Synapse Gap (Mundo Total) *Don't Let A Woman Make A Fool Of You* - Joe King Carrasco + Michael Jackson (Backing Vocals)
LP - MCA 1982

Silk Electric *Muscles*
Diana Ross + Michael Jackson (Writer/Producer)
LP - Capitol 1982

Wolf *So Shy / Papa Was A Rollin' Stone*- Bill Wolfer + Michael Jackson (Backing Vocals)
LP - Constellation 1982

Donna Summer *State of Independence* - Donna Summer + Michael Jackson (Backing Vocals)
LP - Geffen 1982

E.T. Storybook *Someone in the Dark* (Narrated By Michael Jackson)
LP - MCA 1982

Pipes Of Peace *Say, Say, Say / The Man* - Paul McCartney + Michael Jackson (Co-Writer/Vocals)
LP - Columbia 1983

Centipede *Centipede / Come Alive It's Saturday Night* - Rebbie Jackson + Michael Jackson (Writer, Producer And Backing Vocals)
LP - CBS 1984

Dreamstreet *Don't Stand Another Chance* - Janet, Michael & Marlon Jackson
LP - A&M 1984

Dynamite
Tell Me I'm Not Dreamin' (Too Good To Be True) - Jermaine + Michael Jackson (Vocals)
LP - Arista 1984

Somebody's Watching Me
Somebody's Watching Me - Rockwell + Michael Jackson (Vocals)
LP - Motown 1984

Eaten Alive *Eaten Alive* - Diana Ross + Michael Jackson (Co-Writer and Co-Producer)
LP - Capitol 1985

We Are the World *We Are The World* - USA For Africa - Various Artists
LP - CBS 1985

Say You Love Me *You're the One* - Jennifer Holliday + Michael Jackson (Producer and Co-Writer)
LP - Geffen 1985

Pulse *Behind the Mask* Greg Phillinganes + Michael Jackson (Co-Writer)
LP - Planet 1985

August *Behind the Mask* - Eric Clapton + Michael Jackson (Co-Writer)
LP, CD - WEA 1986

Characters *Get It* Stevie Wonder + Michael Jackson (Vocals)
LP - Motown 1987

As Good As It Gets *We Are Here To Change The World* - Deniece Williams + Michael Jackson (Songwriter)
LP - Columbia 1988

Ralph Tresvant *Alright Now* - Ralph Tresvant + Michael Jackson (Co-Writer)
LP, CD - MCA 1990

The Simpsons Sing The Blues *Do the Bartman* - Simpsons + Michael Jackson (Vocals And Co-Producer)
LP, CD - Geffen 1990

I Wasn't Born Yesterday *I Never Heard* - Safire + Michael Jackson (Songwriter)
LP, CD - Mercury 1991

Love's Alright *Whatzupwitu* / *Yeah* - Eddie Murphy + Michael Jackson (Vocals And Backing Vocals)
CD - Motown 1992

Free Willy Soundtrack *Will You Be There* - Various Artists
CD - MJJ 1993

Free Willy 2 Soundtrack *Gone Too Soon* - Various Artists
CD - MJJ 1995

Brotherhood *Brotherhood* / *I Need You* / *Why* - 3T + Michael Jackson (Backing Vocals And Co-Producer)
CD - MJJ 1995

Blackstreet *Joy* - Blackstreet + Michael Jackson (Co-Writer)
CD, Cassette - Interscope 1995

Quo *Quo Funk* - Quo + Michael Jackson (Writer And Backing Vocals)
CD - MJJ 1995

Dreams & Illusions *Mind Is The Magic* - Siegfried & Roy + Michael Jackson (Songwriter, Vocals And Backing Vocals)
CD - Edel 1995

Sunset Park *Keep On Keepin' On* - MC Lyte featuring Xscape + Michael Jackson (Co-Writer)
CD - Flavor Unit 1996

Personal *Personal* - Men Of Vision
CD - MJJ/550 Music/Epic 1996

A Special Part of Me
Love Never Felt So Good - Johnny Mathis + Michael Jackson (Vocals)
CD - CBS 1996

Get On The Bus *On The Line* - Soundtrack album
CD - Epic 1997

COMPILATIONS

Music And Me *With A Child's Heart* / *Up Again* / *All The Things You Are* / *Happy* / *Too Young* / *Doggin' Around* / *Johnny Raven* / *Euphoria* / *Morning Glow* / *Music And Me*
LP - Motown 1973 (CD Reissue 1993)

The Best Of Michael Jackson *Got To Be There* / *Ain't No Sunshine* / *My Girl* / *Ben* / *Greatest Show On Earth* / *I Wanna Be Where You Are* / *Happy* / *Rockin' Robin* / *Just A Little Bit Of You* / *One Day In Your Life* / *Music And Me* / *In Our Small Way* / *We're Almost There* / *Morning Glow*
LP - Motown 1975 (CD Reissue - WD 1985)

One Day In Your Life *One Day In Your Life* / *Don't Say Goodbye Again* / *You're My Best Friend, My Love (Jackson 5)* / *Take Me Back* / *We've Got Forever* / *It's Too Late To Change The Time (Jackson 5)* / *You Are There* / *Dear Michael* / *I'll Come Home To You* / *Make Tonight All Mine (Jackson 5)*
LP - Motown 1981

Ain't No Sunshine *Rockin' Robin* / *Got To Be There* / *Maria (You Were The Only One)* / *You've Got A Friend* / *Girl Don't Take Your Love From Me* / *I Wanna Be Where You Are* / *Don't Let It Get You Down* / *We've Got Forever* / *My Girl* / *Cinderella Stay A While* / *I Like You The Way You Are (Don't Change Your Love On Me)*
LP - Motown 1982

Farewell My Summer Love *Don't Let It Get You Down* / *You've Really Got A Hold On Me* / *Melodie* / *Touch The One You Love* / *Girl You're So Together* / *Farewell My Summer Love* / *Call on Me* / *Here I Am* / *To Make My Father Proud*
LP - Motown 1984 (CD Reissue - WD 1989)

Anthology *Got To Be There* / *Rockin' Robin* / *Ain't No Sunshine* / *Maria (You Were The Only One)* / *I Wanna Be Where You Are* / *Girl Don't Take Your Love From Me* / *Love Is Here And Now You're Gone* / *Ben* / *People Make The World Go 'Round* / *Shoo-Be-Doo-Be-Doo-Da-Day* / *With A Child's Heart* / *Everybody's Somebody's Fool* / *In Our Small Way* / *All The Things You Are* / *You Can Cry On My Shoulder* / *Maybe Tomorrow* / *I'll Be There* / *Never Can Say Goodbye* / *It's Too Late To Change The Time* / *Dancing Machine* / *When I Come Of Age* / *Dear Michael* / *Music And Me* / *You Are There Brown* / *One Day In Your Live* / *Love's Gone Bad* / *That's What Love Is Made Of* / *Who's Looking For A Lover* / *Lonely Teardrops* / *We're Almost There* / *Take Me Back* / *Just A Little Bit Of You* / *Melodie* / *I'll Come Home To You* / *If N' I Was God* / *Happy (Love Theme From "Lady Sings the Blues")* / *Don't Let It Get You Down* / *Call On Me* / *To Make My Father Proud* / *Farewell My Summer Love*
LP, CD - Universal/Motown 1986

Motown Legends *Rockin' Robin* / *Got to Be There* / *Maria (You Were the Only One)* / *You've Got A Friend* / *Girl Don't Take Your Love From Me* / *I Wanna Be Where You Are* / *Don't Let It Get You Down* / *We've Got Forever* / *My Girl* / *Cinderella Stay A While* / *I Like You the Way You Are (Don't Change You Love on Me)*
CD - Universal 1993

Vol. 1 - Greatest Hits HIStory *Billie Jean* / *The Way You Make Me Feel* / *Black or White* / *Rock with You* / *She's Out of My Life* / *Bad* / *I Just Can't Stop Loving You* / *Man In The Mirror* / *Thriller* / *Beat It* / *The Girl Is Mine* / *Remember The Time* / *Don't Stop 'Til You Get Enough* / *Wanna Be Startin' Somethin'* / *Heal The World (Prelude)* / *Heal The World*
CD - Sony/Epic 2001

THE JACKSON 5 ALBUMS

Diana Ross Presents The Jackson 5 *Zip A Dee Doo Dah* / *Nobody* / *I Want You Back* / *Can You Remember* / *Standing In The Shadows Of Love* / *You've Changed* / *My Cherie Amour* / *Who's Loving You* / *Chained* / *(I Know) I'm Losing You* / *Stand* / *Born To Love You*
LP - Motown 1969

ABC *The Love You Save* / *Nobody* / *One More Chance* / *ABC* / *2 4 6 8* / *(Come Round Here) I'm The One You Need* / *Don't Know Why I Love You* / *Never Had A Dream Come True* / *True Love Can Be Beautiful* / *La La Means I Love You* / *Stand* / *I'll Bet You* / *I Found That Girl* / *The Young Folks*
LP - Motown 1970

The Christmas Album *Have Yourself A Merry Little Christmas* / *Santa Claus Is Comin' To Town* / *The Christmas Song* / *Up On The House Top* / *Frosty The Snowman* / *The Little Drummer Boy* / *Rudolph The Red Nosed Reindeer* / *Christmas Won't Be The Same This Year* / *Give Love On Christmas Day* / *Someday At Christmas* / *I Saw Mommy Kissing Santa Claus*
LP - Motown 1970

The Third Album *I'll Be There / Ready Or Not (Here I Come) / Oh How Happy / Bridge Over Troubled Water / Can I See You In The Morning / Goin' Back To Indiana / How Funky Is Your Chicken / Mama's Pearl / Reach In / The Love I Saw In You Was Just A Mirage / Darling Dear*
LP - Motown 1971

Maybe Tomorrow *Maybe Tomorrow / She's Good / Never Can Say Goodbye / The Wall / Petals / 16 Candles / (We've Got) Blue Skies / My Little Baby / It's Great To Be Here / Honey Chile / I Will Find A Way*
LP - Motown 1971

Goin' Back To Indiana *I Want You Back / Maybe Tomorrow / The Day Basketball Was Saved / Stand / I Want To Take You Higher / Feelin' Alright / Walk On / The Love You Save / Goin' Back To Indiana*
LP - Motown 1972

The Greatest Hits *I Want You Back / ABC / Never Can Say Goodbye / Sugar Daddy / I'll Be There / Maybe Tomorrow / The Love You Save / Who's Lovin You / Mama's Pearl / Goin' Back To Indiana / I Found That Girl*
LP - Motown 1972

Looking Through The Windows *Ain't Nothing Like The Real Thing / Lookin' Through The Windows / Doctor My Eyes / Little Bitty Pretty One / E-Ne-Me-Ne-Mi-Ne-Moe / If I Have To Move A Mountain / Children Of The Light / I Can Only Give You Love*
LP - Motown 1972

Skywriter *Skywriter / Hallelujah Day / The Boogie Man / Touch / Corner Of The Sky / I Can't Quit Your Love / Uppermost / World Of Sunshine / Ooh, I'd Love To Be With You / You Made Me What I Am Today*
LP - Motown 1973

Get It Together *Get It Together / Don't Say Goodbye Again / Reflections / Hum Along And Dance / Mama I Got A Brand New Thing (Don't Say No) / It's Too Late To Change The Time / You Need Love Like I Do (Don't You?) / Dancing Machine*
LP - Motown 1973

Dancing Machine *I Am Love / Whatever You Got, I Want / She's A Rhythm Child / Dancing Machine / The Life Of The Party / What You Don't Know / If I Don't Love You This Way / It All Begins And Ends With Love / The Mirrors Of My Mind*
LP - Motown 1974

Moving Violation *Forever Came Today / Moving Violation / (You Were Made) Especially For Me / Honey Love / Body Language (Do The Love Dance) / All I Do Is Think Of You / Breezy / Call Of The Wild / Time Explosion*
LP - Motown 1975

Joyful Jukebox Music *Joyful Jukebox Music / Window Shopping / You're My Best Friend, My Love / Love Is The Thing You Need / The Eternal Light / Pride And Joy / Through Thick And Thin / We're Here To Entertain You / We're Gonna Change Our Style*
LP - Motown 1976

Millennium Collection-20th Century Masters *I Want You Back / ABC / The Love You Save / I'll Be There / Never Can Say Goodbye / Got To Be There / Sugar Daddy / Daddy's Home / I Wanna Be Where You Are / Maybe Tomorrow / Dancing Machine*
CD - Universal/Motown 1995

Pre-History: The Ripples & Waves Plus Michael *Let Me Carry Your Schoolbooks / I Never Had A Girl / The Lover / We Don't Have To Be Over 21 / Big Boy / You've Changed / Jam Session / My Girl / Under The Boardwalk / Soul Jerk / Saturday Night At The Movies / Tracks Of My Tears*
LP - Steeltown 1968 (CD Reissue - Brunswick 1996)

Anthology (Disc 1) *I Want You Back / Who's Loving You / ABC / The Young Folks / The Love You Save / I Found That Girl / I'll Bet You / I'll Be There / Goin' Back To Indiana / Mama's Pearl / Darling Dear / Never Can Say Goodbye / Maybe Tomorrow / It's Great To Be Here / Sugar Daddy / I'm So Happy / Medley: Sing A Simple Song/Can You Remember - At The Hollywood Palace / Doctor My Eyes / Little Bitty Pretty One / Lookin' Through The Windows / Love Song - (Disc 2) Corner Of The Sky / Touch / Hallelujah Day / Daddy's Home (J5 Live In Japan) / Get It Together / Hum Along And Dance / Mama I Gotta' Brand New Thing (Don't Say No) / It's Too Late To Change The Time / Dancing Machine (Original LP Version) / Whatever You Got, I Want / The Life Of The Party / I Am Love / All I Do Is Think Of You / Forever Came Today / We're Here To Entertain You*
Double CD - Universal / Motown 2000

THE JACKSON 5 SINGLES

I Want You Back *I Want You Back / Who's Loving You*
7" - Motown 1970

ABC *ABC / The Young Folks*
7" - Motown 1970

The Love You Save *The Love You Save / I Found That Girl*
7" - Motown 1970

I'll Be There *I'll Be There / One More Chance*
7" - Motown 1970

Mama's Pearl *Mama's Pearl / Darling Dear*
7" - Motown 1971

Never Can Say Goodbye *Never Can Say Goodbye / She's Good*
7" - Motown 1971

Maybe Tomorrow *Maybe Tomorrow*
7" - Motown 1971

Sugar Daddy *Sugar Daddy / I'm So Happy*
7" - Motown 1972

Little Bitty Pretty One *Little Bitty Pretty One / Maybe Tomorrow*
7" - Motown 1972

Lookin' Through The Windows *Lookin' Through The Windows / Love Song*
7" - Motown 1972

Santa Claus Is Coming To Town *Santa Claus Is Coming To Town / Someday At Christmas / Christmas Won't Be The Same This Year*
7" - Motown 1972

Corner Of The Sky *Corner Of The Sky*
7" - Motown 1972

Hallelujah Day *Hallelujah Day / To Know*
7" - Motown 1973

Doctor My Eyes *Doctor My Eyes / My Little Baby*
7" - Motown 1973

Skywriter *Skywriter / Ain't Nothing Like The Real Thing*
7" - Motown 1973

Get It Together *Get It Together / Touch*
7" - Motown 1973

The Boogie Man *The Boogie Man / Don't Let Your Baby Catch You*
7" - Motown 1974

Whatever You Got, I Want *Whatever You Got, I Want*
7" - Motown 1974

Dancing Machine *Dancing Machine / It's Too Late To Change The Time*
7" - Motown 1974

Life Of The Party *Life Of The Party / Whatever You've Got, I Want*
7" - Motown 1974

I Am Love *I Am Love Pt. 1 / I Am Love Pt. 2*
7" - Motown 1975

Forever Came Today *Forever Came Today / I Can't Quit Your Love*
7" - Motown 1975

Skywriter *Skywriter / I Want You Back / The Love You Save*
7" - Motown 1977

I Want You Back *I Want You Back / The Love You Save*
7" - Motown 1980

I'll Be There *I'll Be There / ABC*
7" - Motown 1980

Looking Through The Windows *Looking Through The Windows / Doctor My Eyes*
7" - Motown 1980

THE JACKSON 5 WITH OTHERS

Motown At The Hollywood Palace *Sing A Simple Song*
LP - Motown 1970

Diana! *Walk On By*
LP - Motown 1971

Jermaine *That's How Love Goes* - Jermaine Jackson + Jackson 5 (Backing Vocals)
LP - Motown 1972

A Motown Christmas (Various Artists) *Little Christmas Tree*
LP - Motown 1973

Fulfillingness' First Finale *You Haven't Done Nothing* - Stevie Wonder + Jackson 5 (Backing Vocals)
LP - Motown 1974

THE JACKSONS - ALBUMS

The Jacksons *Enjoy Yourself / Think Happy / Good Times / Keep On Dancing / Blues Away / Show You The Way To Go / Living Together / Strength Of One Man / Dreamer / Style Of Life*
LP - Epic 1976

Goin' Places *Music's Taking Over / Goin' Places / Different Kind Of Lady / Even Though You're Gone / Jump For Joy / Heaven Knows I Love You, Girl / Man Of War / Do What You Wanna / Find Me A Girl*
LP - Epic 1977

Destiny *Blame It On The Boogie / Push Me Away / Things I Do For You / Shake Your Body (Down To The Ground) / Destiny / Bless His Soul / All Night Dancin' / That's What You Get (For Being Polite)*
LP - Epic 1978

Triumph *Can You Feel It / Lovely One / Your Ways / Everybody / This Place Hotel / Walk Right Now / Give It Up / Wondering Who*
LP - Epic 1980

Live *Opening/Can You Feel It / Things I Do For You / Off The Wall / Ben / This Place Hotel / She's Out Of My Life / Movie & Rap, Incl.I Want You Back/Never Can Say Goodbye/Got To Be There / Medley Incl. I Want You Back/ABC/The Love You Save / I'll Be There / Rock With You / Lovely One / Working Day And Night / Don't Stop 'Til You Get Enough*
LP - Epic 1981

Victory *Torture / Wait / One More Chance / Be Not Always / State Of Shock / We Can Chance The World / The Hurt / Body*
LP - Epic 1984

2300 Jackson Street *Art Of Madness / Nothin' (That Compares To You) / Maria / Private Affair / 2300 Jackson Street / Harley / She / Alright With Me / Play It Up / Midnight Rendezvous / If You'd Only Believe*
LP - Epic 1989

THE JACKSONS - SINGLES

Enjoy Yourself *Enjoy Yourself / Style Of Life*
7" - Epic 1976

Show You The Way To Go *Show You The Way To Go / Blues Ways*
7" - Epic 1977

Dreamer *Dreamer / Good Times*
7" - Epic 1977

Goin' Places *Goin' Places / Do What You Wanna*
7" - Epic 1977

Even Though You're Gone *Even Though You're Gone / Different Kind Of Lady*
7" - Epic 1978

Music's Taking Over *Music's Taking Over / Man Of War*
7" - Epic 1978

Blame It On The Boogie *Blame It On The Boogie / Do What You Wanna*
7" - Epic 1978

Destiny *Destiny / That's What You Get (For Being Polite)*
7" - Epic 1978

Destiny *Destiny / Blame It On The Boogie / That's What You Get (For Being Polite)*
12" - Epic 1978

Shake Your Body Down To The Ground *Shake Your Body Down To The Ground / All Night Dancing*
7", 12" - Epic 1979

Lovely One *Lovely One / The Things I Do For You*
7" - Epic 1980

Heartbreak Hotel *Heartbreak Hotel / Different Kind Of Lady*
7" - Epic 1980

Can You Feel It *Can You Feel It / Wonderin' Who*
7" - Epic 1981

Can You Feel It *Can You Feel It / Wonderin' Who / Shake Your Body*
12" - Epic 1981

Walk Right Now *Walk Right Now / Your Ways*
7", 12" - Epic 1981

Time Waits For No One *Time Waits For No One / Give It Up*
7" - Epic 1981

The Things I Do For You *The Things I Do For You / Don't Stop Til You Get Enough*
7" - Epic 1981

State Of Shock *State Of Shock* (With Mick Jagger) / *Your Ways*
7", 12" - Epic 1981

Show You The Way To Go *Show You The way To Go* / *Blame It On The Boogie*
7" - Epic 1984

DVD AND VIDEO

The Wiz Feature film musical black adaptation of *The Wonderful Wizard Of Oz* with Michael Jackson as the Scarecrow and Diana Ross as Dorothy.
VHS - Universal 1982 (DVD Reissue - Universal 1999)

The Making Of Michael Jackson's Thriller Starring Michael Jackson and directed by John Landis. Includes the videos for *Can You Feel It, Thriller, Beat It, Billie Jean*, and footage of Michael's live performance of *Billie Jean* at Motown 25.
VHS - Universal 1983

Motown 25: Yesterday, Today And Forever Video recording of the 1983 Motown reunion concert as well as a look behind the scenes of the label. Includes live performance by The Jackson 5 and Michael's Emmy nominated performance of Billie Jean
VHS - Movis 1983

We Are The World: USA For Africa Behind the scenes look at the recording of the famine relief song. Narrated by Jane Fonda.
VHS - Musicvision / RCA Columbia Pictures 1985

Grammy's Greatest Moments V. 1 Charity video release for Musicares charity of the 30th Grammy Awards, 2nd March 1988. Jackson performs *The Way You Make Me Feel* and *Man In The Mirror*.
VHS - WEA 1988

Moonwalker Full-length feature film with montage of old Jackson video clips, live performances and new 'fantasy' videos - with Joe Pesci and Sean Lennon.
VHS - MJJ/Epic 1988

Michael Jackson: The Legend Continues Television special about Michael from Motown days to solo career.
VHS - Optimum Productions 1989

Dangerous: The Short Films *Black Or White, In The Closet, Heal The World, Jam, Remember The Time, Give In To Me, Gone Too Soon, Will You Be There, Who Is It* - also tour profiles and making of the music videos.
VHS, Laser Disc - Epic 1993 (DVD Reissue - Epic 2000)

Video Greatest Hits: HIStory *Brace Yourself / Billie Jean / The Way You Make Me Feel / Black Or White / Rock With You / BAD / Thriller / Beat It / Remember The Time / Don't Stop 'Til You Get Enough / Heal The World* - DVD version also includes 18-minute version of the music video for Bad directed by Martin Scorsese
VHS - UPC 1995 (DVD Reissue 2000)

HIStory On Film: Volume II *HIStory Teaser / Billie Jean Motown 25 Performance / Beat It / Liberian Girl / Smooth Criminal / 1995 MTV Video Music Awards Performance / Thriller/ Scream / Childhood / You Are Not Alone / Earth Song / They Don't Care About Us (Rio Version) / Stranger In Moscow / Dance Megamix / Brace Yourself / Blood On The Dance Floor (Refugee's Camp Mix Version)*
VHS - UPC 1997

Ghosts Music, dance and special effects extravaganza directed by Stan Winston and written by Mick Garris on an original idea by Michael Jackson and Stephen King. Originally screened in Sony movie theatres and at film festivals including Palm Springs and Cannes.
VHS - Sony 1997

BOOTLEGS

Bootlegs are unofficial releases of mixes, live recordings, downloads and rare tracks. There are numerous such items around featuring Michael Jackson and below are a selection of the most common ones. It should be noted that to sell or trade in bootleg material is a criminal offence, therefore they are only available from underground sources such as market stalls and record fairs. The authors and publishers of the book do not endorse any trade in such items nor do they have any further information about their availability.

Love At Last - The Complete Rarities Collection*The Way You Make Me Feel (1988 Grammy Awards) / I Want You Back (Prelude)/I Want You Back/The Love You Save/Never Can Say Goodbye/I'll Be There/Billy Jean (Motown's 25th Anniversary Show) / Come Together (from Moonwalker) / Ease On Down The Road (Live With Diana Ross) / Jam/Billie Jean/Black Or White (The Superbowl XXV11 Half Time Show) / Get It (Disco Remix With Stevie Wonder) / I'll Be There (Presentation Mix) / You Were There (Live & Unrecorded Dedicated To Sammy Davis) / Todo Mi Amor Eres Tu (I Can't Stop Loving You) / Blame It On The Boogie (Extended Disco Mix) / Shake Your Body (Extended Disco Remix) / Enjoy Yourself (12" Extended Version) / Thriller (Long Dance Version) / The Way You Make Me Feel (Dance Remix Radio Edit)*

Michael Jackson King Of Pop - The Mystery Of HIStory *Intro / Scream / They Don't Care About Us / In The Closet / Wanna Be Startin' Something / Stranger In Moscow / Smooth Criminal / You Are Not Alone / I Want You Back / Doctor Love / I'll Be There / Billie Jean / Thriller / Beat It / Blood On The Dance Floor / Dangerous / Black Or White / Earth Song / Heal The World / They Don't Care About Us / History / 2 Bad / Dance Part / Is It Scary / Ghost* - Double CD Set.
All recorded live at the Olympic Stadium, Munich July 1997.

He Drives Me Wild - The Rare Promo Mixes Vol 1 *Smooth Criminal (DMC Remix) / Dirty Diana (DMC Remix) / Liberian Girl (DMC Remix) / Bad (DMC Remix) / The Way You Make Me Feel (French Disco Version) / Jam (Ted Riley Remix) / Jam (A Cappella) / Black Or White (Remix) / The Man (Extended Versions) / Someone In The Dark (Unreleased) / Someone Put Your Hand Out (Unreleased Promo) / Dangerous Medley (Unreleased Promo) / You Can't Win (Disco Remix) / You Can't Get Out Of The Rain (Version)*

He Still Drives Me Wild - The Rare Promo Mixes Vol 2 *Way You Make Me Feel/Billie Jean/Bad/Thriller/Don't Stop/Shake Your Body/Wanna Be Startin' Something/Beat It (Disco Mix Club Remixes) / Thriller/Bad/Don't Stop/Rock With You/Billie Jean/Thriller (Reprise)/Thriller/ Smooth Criminal (Disco Club Remix) / Criminal Heart (Michael Jackson and Rick Astley, Annie & Brother Mix / Smooth Criminal (Smokin' Gun Mix) / Human Nature (12" Remix) / Speed Demon (Disco Mix Club Remix) / Billie Jean/Rock With You/Burn This Disco Out/Off The Wall/Don't*

Stop/Shake Your Body/Blame It On The Boogie/Thriller/Billie Jean (Disco Mix Club Compilation Mix) / Remember The Time (The Ultimate Mix)

Michael Jackson: Great Duets & Unreleased Demos Todo Mi Amor Eres Tu (I Can't Stop Loving You With Siedah Garrett / Save Me (With Dave Mason) / Ease On Down The Road (12" Version With Diana Ross) / The Man (With Paul McCartney) / Goin' Back To Alabama (With Kenny Rogers) / Just Friends (With Carole Bayer Sager) / You're The One (With Jennifer Holliday) / Get It (Special 12" Version With Stevie Wonder) / Jam (Unreleased Vocal Demo Version) / Give In To Me (Unreleased Instrumental Version) / Someone Put Your Hand Out (Promo Cassette Version)

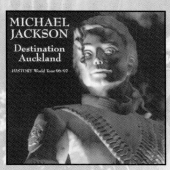

Michael Jackson: Destination Auckland
Golden Gates / Scream / They Don't Care About Us / In The Closet / Smooth Criminal / The Way You Make Me Feel / I Want You Back / The Love You Save / I'll Be There / Rock With You/Off The Wall/Don't Stop / Billie Jean / Thriller / Beat It / Black Or White / Earth Song / History - All Tracks Recorded Live At Ericsson Stadium, Auckland, NZ 9.11.96

Michael Jackson King Of Pop (Special Guest Sade) Black Or White (The C&C House Club Remix) / Remember The Time (New Main Mix) / Remember The Time (A Cappella, Remix By NJs Future Team) / In The Closet (The Reprise) / In The Closet (Underground Remix) / Who Is It (Lake Side Dub) / Who Is It (Moby's Raw Mercy Dub) / Jam (Silky 7 Inch) / Jam (Roger's Jeep Mix) / Give In To Me (Vocal Version)/ Smooth Operator (Version 1 Michael With Sade) / Smooth Operator (Version 2 Michael With Sade)

BOOKS AND AUDIO BOOKS

Michael!
by Mark Bego
Pinnacle Books 1984

On The Road With Michael!
by Mark Bego
Pinnacle Books 1984

Michael Jackson Body And Soul: An Illustrated Biography
by Geoff Brown
Beaufort Books 1984

The Michael Jackson Story
by Nelson George
Dell 1984

Michael Jackson
by Robin Katz
Gallery Books/W.H.Smith 1984

Michael Jackson: Thrill
by Caroline Latham
Zebra Books 1984

This Is Michael Jackson
by D.L. Mabery
Lerner Publications 1984

The Michael Jackson Catalog: A Comprehensive Guide To Records, Videos, Clothing, Posters, Toys & Millions Of Collectible Souvenirs
by Milt Machlin
Morrow 1984

Michael Jackson
by Gordon Matthews
Wanderer Books 1984

The Totally Unauthorized Michael Jackson Trivia Book
by Mark Rowland
Tom Doherty Associates 1984

Trapped: Michael Jackson And The Crossover Dream
by Dave Marsh
Bantam Books 1985

We Are The World
by David Breskin
Perigee 1985

Sequins & Shades: The Michael Jackson Reference Guide
by Carol Terry
Pierian Press 1986

Moonwalker - The Storybook
by Michael Jackson
Doubleday 1988

My Family, The Jacksons
by Katherine Jackson with Richard Wiseman
St. Martin's Paperbacks 1990

Michael Jackson: Music's Living Legend
by Rosemary Wallner
Abdo and Daughters 1991

Michael Jackson: The Magic And The Madness
by J. Randy Taraborrelli
Ballantine Books 1991

Dancing The Dream: Poems And Reflections
by Michael Jackson
Doubleday 1992

Michael Jackson: Live & Dangerous
by Adrian Grant
Omnibus Press 1992

Michael Jackson: King Of Pop
by Chris Cardell
Jam Books 1992

In His Own Words: Michael Jackson
by Catherine Dineen
Omnibus Press 1993

Michael Jackson: The King Of Pop
by Lisa D. Campbell
Branden Publishing 1993

Michael Jackson: The King Of Pop's Darkest Hour
by Lisa D. Campbell
Branden Publishing 1994

Michael Jackson: A Visual Documentary
by Adrian Grant
Omnibus Press 1994

Michael Jackson: Dangerous
by Carol Cuellar (Editor)
Warner Brothers Publications 1994

Michael Jackson Unauthorized
by Christopher P. Andersen
Simon & Schuster Publishing 1994

Michael Jackson: Entertainer
by Lois P. Nicholson, Coretta Scott King (Introduction)
Main Line Book Co. 1994

Michael Jackson
by Lois P. Nicholson
Demco Media 1994

Michael Jackson - History: Past, Present, and Future
edited by Sy Feldman
Warner Brothers Publications 1995

Jackson Family Values
by Margaret Maldonado Jackson with Richard Hack
Dove Books 1995

"I Can't Believe It! Michael Jackson": Michael Be Strong
by Telia Diane Perryman
Dorrance Publishing Company, Inc. 1996

Michael Jackson, American Master
by C. Mecca
CAM Publishing 1996

Michael Jackson CD Book
Music Book Services Corporation 1996

The Many Faces Of Michael Jackson
by Lee Pinkerton
Ozone Books 1998

Michael Jackson: Making History
by Adrian Grant
Omnibus Press 1998

Loving Michael Jackson
by Selena Millman
Biographical Pub Co. 2001

The Michael Jackson Collection
by Bill Nation
Warner Brothers Publications, 2001

Michael Jackson (People In The News)
by Karen Marie Graves
Lucent Books 2001

Maximum Michael Jackson
The Unauthorised Audio Biography by Darren Brooks
Chrome Dreams 2001

JACKSON ON THE WEB

For sourcing additional information about Michael Jackson, you really can't beat the World Wide Web. There are numerous sites about Michael Jackson containing a wide range of biographical information, pictures, up-to-the-minute news and tour dates as well as MP3's of both his well known and rarer tracks. The following sites are among the most comprehensive and a good place to start finding out about Michael Jackson online. Search engines such as Yahoo and Google can uncover many more fan sites. Up-to-date information can also be found on general music sites such as www.rollingstone.com, www.nme.com, www.mtv.com and www.getmusic.com.

www.michaeljackson.com - Official Site

www.mjsite.com

www.m-jackson.com

www.mjworld.net

www.planetjackson.com

www.mjfanclub.net

www.exclusivelymj.com

www.michaeljackson.net

www.mjackson.com

www.healtheworld.com

PHOTO CREDITS

Photos Courtesy of:
Rex Features London • London Features • Redferns
Reproductions of record/CD artwork courtesy of Sony, Epic and Motown Records.